SAVE
BRITAIN'S HERITAGE

presents

Historic Naval & Military Architecture

This report and accompanying exhibition have been generously sponsored by:

ENGLISH HERITAGE

HAMPSHIRE COUNTY COUNCIL

THE JOHN AND RUTH HOWARD CHARITABLE TRUST

THE ROYAL OAK FOUNDATION through a gift from **THE DRUE HEINZ FOUNDATION**

The exhibition and the cover of this book have been designed by Robin Ollington who has generously designed previous exhibitions and SAVE reports on a voluntary basis.

SAVE particularly wishes to thank Jonathan Coad, Andrew Saunders, Brigadier Hamilton Baillie, Iain MacIvor, Ian Gailey, Roger Bowdler and Bill Bolger for their constant help with this project.

Further assistance has come from Jane Alexander, James Arnott, Edward Batholomew, Reg Betts, Anthony Cantwell, Peter Cobb, Major R S Cross, Col Henry Day, Duncan Gillard, Mary Hatwell, Historic Scotland, Capt D D Horn, Major A W Kersting, Anthony Lake, T M Lewin & Sons, The Light Infantry, Tom & Juliet Lloyd, the late Anthony Lowther-Pinkerton, David Moore, Nick Moore, the National Maritime Museum, the O'Shea Gallery, Portsmouth Naval Base Property Trust, Judy Prendergast, Gordon Smith, Victor Smith, Roger Thomas, Julian Wakeham, Major W H White, Freddie Woodward, Zephyr Flags.

SAVE also wishes to thank Jill Lever and her staff at the RIBA Heinz Gallery for their help in preparing the exhibition **Deserted Bastions**.

NOTE: This report is based on extensive research but does not claim to be comprehensive. The Gazeteer concentrates on buildings in three principle categories. First: those that have been demolished, second: those that have closed, may soon close or are possible candidates for closure, and third: those that have been preserved for the public to visit or adapted to alternative use.

The major part of both the historical research and the picture research for the exhibition and the gazeteer has been carried out by SAVE's caseworker, Anthony Peers.

ISBN 0 905978 31 5

Published April 1993

68 Battersea High Street
London SW11 3HX
Tel: 071 228 3336

Edited by Marianne Watson-Smyth

Printed by The Book Factory, London N7

DESERTED BASTIONS

Historic Naval & Military Architecture

Contents

DESERTED BASTIONS

Historic Naval and Military Architecture

Introduction by Marcus Binney

Over nearly twenty years the SAVE spotlight has been turned on successive areas of Britain's vanishing heritage - first country houses, then railway stations, followed by textile mills, nonconformist chapels, hospitals and asylums, pubs and public baths, barns and pumping stations - and now the legacy of the army, navy and airforce.

The purpose in every case is to show the remarkable range of buildings that survive, to highlight those that are in danger and to illustrate imaginative new uses.

While prehistoric hill forts and medieval castles are well known and usually well protected, the defence heritage of later centuries is much less studied. Partly because much of it is the work of military and naval engineers rather than architects, little of it appears in the classics of architectural history such as Summerson's Architecture in Britain, Colvin's Dictionary of British Architects and Pevsner's History of Building Types. Popular books like the Shell Guide to England and the Readers' Digest volume The Past All Around Us cover the agricultural and industrial heritage, coal, iron, canals and follies but give even Regency Sandhurst only a passing mention.

In recent years the work of Brigadier Hamilton-Baillie and the Fortress Study Group and of Jonathan Coad and Andrew Saunders (all of whom contribute to this report) has documented the extraordinary range of post-medieval defensive architecture. This includes not just barracks and dockyards, but a whole alphabet of intriguing structures- arsenals and armouries, boathouses and breweries, casemates and caponiers, rigging houses and roperies, sawmills and smitheries.

Now defence cutbacks following the end of the Cold War, combined with general government economies, mean many substantial defence establishments face possible closure. The list of redundancies is far from definite and is likely to be hotly contested, even more from within than without. In some cases the return of troops from Germany may even prompt the refurbishment of barracks that have been disused.

But there are also many sites which have been closed or virtually closed for some years, such as Woolwich Arsenal and Pembroke Dock.

This report and exhibition therefore appear at a time of positive turmoil. There are, it is estimated, over a thousand listed structures on the Defence estate; this compares with 1,073 listed structures belonging to British Rail and an even larger number on the National Health Service estate.

Happily, for all the necessary emphasis on the most up to date technology and equipment, pride in this heritage within the Forces remains extremely strong. The Gunners are to retain their great shrine at Woolwich - the single longest Georgian composition in the country, dwarfing even the great facade of Wentworth Woodhouse. Proof of this comes in the scaffold, erected the entire length of the main south facade two months ago.

Though the scale of potential redundancy is alarming, the scope for new uses is enormous, and thanks to positive initiatives from government much has already been achieved. Michael Heseltine established Dockyard Trusts at Chatham and Portsmouth with substantial cash dowries and £50 million has been provided by government to breathe new life into the Royal William Yard at Devonport, Plymouth. Chatham and Portsmouth, despite major teething problems, are well on their way to becoming two of the nation's top tourist attractions.

At the other end of the scale is the Royal Ordnance Depot at Weedon in Northamptonshire. This is a remarkable series of munitions stores ranged on either side of a canal like Louis XIV's long lost palace at Marly and glimpsed fleetingly from the train as it approaches Rugby.

Weedon, which seemed the biggest white elephant of all, was bought by an entrepreneur with a major furniture export business. He had been about to build a new £500,000 warehouse when he discovered he could buy the whole of the ordnance depot for less than twice the price. Now Weedon hums to the tune of saws and forklift trucks and the heavy duty lifts in the munition stores shift furniture rather than shells.

Huge interest in military history means that many of the best buildings and sites can be successfully opened to the public. The Ministry of Defence and Historic Scotland have set an example with Fort George near Inverness, immaculately restoring the buildings and opening the Fort to the public while it remains in military use. Hampshire County Council have taken an impressive lead by acquiring and opening sites such as Fort Nelson.

The vast hangar at Cardington, Bedfordshire, built for the R100 airship, said to be the largest enclosed space in Britain, has recently been adapted by the Building Research Institute as a place where modern buildings and building materials can be tested to destruction. Meanwhile the external corrugated iron sheeting is being restored from end to end at a cost of £4 million.

There is also a potential marriage, which government ministers must foster, between major defence buildings and polytechnics recently granted university status such as Plymouth and Portsmouth. Woolwich Arsenal is equally a possible site for the new University of Greenwich. In Seville, the university has long been handsomely housed in the splendid eighteenth century royal tobacco factory. Great naval buidings such as the symmetrical ranges of Royal William Yard have similar potential.

SAVE's report, Chatham Dockyard: Alive or Mothballed, prepared with the entrepreneur Kit Martin, showed how very large dockyard buildings could be sympathetically adapted to residential use on a commercial basis, without changing their external appearance and retaining many internal features. In the event, Chatham Dockyard was vested in a preservation trust but the solution proposed can - and should - be applied to other military and naval buildings, illustrated in this report.

Alternative use inevitably brings a degree of change, but the Admiral Hotel in Copenhagen, converted from a vast eighteenth century granary, shows how sympathetically this can be done. Externally not one window has been changed and inside all the massive baltic timbers, both posts and beams, have been retained, and are seen in majestic perspective in the public spaces on the ground floor. They reappear in every bedroom, while still meeting modern safety regulations.

Sir John Smith, founder of The Landmark Trust, and restorer of HMS Warrior, has repeatedly said that most problem historic buildings are not in financial trouble but in legal trouble - crippled by a stalemate over terms of sale or lease, means of access and curtilage or amenity land.

Ministers have rightly put pressure on government departments and public bodies to sell buildings and land they no longer require. Clearly it is desirable that they should be sold quickly while they are in good condition. Most, though not all, historic buildings on the defence estate, have been well maintained while in use and quite a number have been sensibly mothballed when vacated to ensure they don't deteriorate. A good example is the Horseshoe Barracks at Shoeburyness.

SAVE's experience in dealing with the whole spectrum of historic buildings is that the key to a satisfactory solution lies in the setting as much as the historic building itself.

If the building has sufficient land to protect it, to provide a reasonable degree of privacy and amenity, it will be possible to find a new owner or a new use. But if the immediate surroundings are parcelled off for development and sold, or spoiled in some other way, the chances of finding a viable solution will diminish and the amount of public money involved in saving the building will dramatically increase.

Here there is a major problem with the procedures laid down in the Treasury's memorandum on the disposal of land and buildings. The consistent theme of this paper is that government bodies must obtain, and be seen to obtain, the highest price for every property sold, and in most cases to explore development value before marketing the building.

Holding out for the highest possible price, as every seller knows, can simply deprive one of a sale while costs of maintenance continue to clock up. The Treasury encourages public bodies to make applications for outline planning permission but as these are by nature speculative, they are likely to run into strong local opposition, thereby delaying or even paralysing the process of disposal.

Where an application for planning permission conflicts with established planning policies or green belt or AONB designations, opposition is likely to come from District and County Councils, official bodies with an interest in protecting the character of town and countryside as well as local people.

With redundant historic buildings, the first move should be to decide how much land and what access is needed to make reuse a viable proposition, and then to work out what other parts of the site can be developed sympathetically. The production of a responsible masterplan, rather than a blueprint for a carve-up is much more likely to win support and speed disposal.

The second weakness of the Treasury memorandum is the insistence of going out to tender on any large site. While it sounds a plausible approach, the reality is that an entrepreneur entering such a tendering procedure will be involved in very substantial costs. In almost every case, what is required by the government body involved is not just a cash offer, but quite detailed plans and costings. The entrepreneurs themselves will want to make their own evaluations of feasibility, use and cost. All this will usually involve tens of thousands of pounds in fees. Yet at best the chances of acquiring the property in such circumstances will be one in three and there will always be the chance that the public body will change its mind and decide not to sell at all. For anybody with experience and a successful track record in converting historic buildings, there are much more attractive propositions available.

The result is that the takers of large and architecturally important defence buildings are likely to be of two types. First is the speculator, whose basic interest is to make a turn by buying the property, obtaining planning permission or some kind of in-principle planning approval, and selling it on immediately at a profit. The second is the volume housebuilder who has an interest in obtaining open ground on which to build housing. In both cases the result is likely to be a carve up of the site, leaving the historic part of the complex with too little land to make it a viable proposition.

Yet sold to the right people on reasonable terms, even the largest historic buildings can take on an important new role, often contributing significantly to the regeneration of a run down area or even the whole town. One classic example is Dean Clough Mills in Halifax. This consisted of 1.5 million square feet of derelict industrial space, much of it in 19th century textile mills up to ten storeys high. Ernest Hall had a vision of transforming it into nursery space for small businesses. Dean Clough now houses over 200 small firms with a total workforce of almost 1500. Well over half the total space is occupied by small enterprises ranging from car repairing to printing, computer sales and design. Now major insurance companies and even the local VAT office have moved in.

Another successful example is the Royal Victoria Patriotic Asylum on Wandsworth Common in London. Here another entrepreneur has breathed new life into every part of the complex with virtually no external changes. The majority of the buildings have become offices and apartments while the great hall is a school of theatre and dance.

Britain's military and naval heritage also extends overseas. In the Channel Islands both Alderney and Jersey have spectacular breakwaters, begun as part of a plan to create giant harbours of refuge where the British home fleet could anchor menacingly off Cherbourg. Their construction was prompted by fears that the new railway link from Paris to Cherbourg would enable the French to land tens of thousands of troops on England's south coast within 24 hours. Then dawned the realisation that tiny Alderney was itself a prey to invasion and that the new harbour could easily be taken by the French. So the island was fortified with a remarkable series of 22 forts and batteries built by the Victorian military engineer Captain Jervois, with a host of intriguing medieval detail. These are British fortifications which it is quite beyond the means of a small island with a population of 2,000 to preserve. Yet the potential is shown by the Landmark Trust which has taken over Fort Clonque and restored it as one of its most unusual and popular holiday lets.

Our own publication, SAVE Gibraltar's Heritage, was the first wide ranging study of the whole spectrum of military and naval building on the Rock, containing a list of 1100 buildings and structures of historic and architectural interest. One of the Hong Kong islands contains a remarkable series of Victorian casemates similar to those at Dover and Portsmouth. As well as Nelson's Dockyard in Antigua a remarkable collection of British naval buildings is to be found in the Simonstown naval base near Capetown.

The world over, from Savannah to San Francisco and Sydney, quays and dockside warehouses have been transformed into flourishing quarters of shops, cafes and restaurants. Some people affect to despise tourism but it is now the world's largest industry, with enormous potential for growth. SAVE, in Preservation Pays, showed that in 1977 historic buildings and areas were responsible for earning at the very minimum, some £500 million in foreign exchange. Again at the minimum, SAVE calculated that at least £60 million of this accrued directly to central government through VAT and duty on petrol, liquor and cigarettes. By contrast the total available in annual grants by the Historic Buildings Council for England was £4.6 million. This was at a time when VAT was 8% rather than today's 17.5%.

In recent years, the heritage of the armed forces has provided the raison d'etre for some of Britain's liveliest museums: the Tank Museum at Bovingdon, the displays at Chatham Dockyard, the RAF Museum at Hendon and the Imperial War Museum's outstation at Duxford.

The point that has emerged most strongly from SAVE's researches is the enormous wealth of interest and affection for these places among those that have served in the armed forces or encountered them on national service and in the Territorial Army.

And while the size of some of these buildings and sites is intimidating it is worth remembering that on the continent there are still larger historic military installations in still more desperate need of repair. At Josefov in Bohemia, the former Imperial Barracks cover an area similar in size to the City of London's square mile, with street after street of four and five storey buildings. The complex was given a new lease of life (of a sort) after the Soviet army invaded Czechoslavakia in 1968 and built a Berlin style wall across the middle to create a sealed compound.

The new Czech republic is faced with finding new uses for dozens and dozens of hastily vacated military installations, many of them centred on fine historic country houses and castles. Peering over the padlocked gates at Zechovice I gained a glimpse of an eighteenth century house last Spring. I was suddenly approached by a man in a boiler suit. "I'm the mayor" he said, producing the keys "Let me show you round. We want to sell it as a hotel. I'll give you our marketing video". This is precisely the spirit of enterprise needed to breathe life into the extraordinary range of fine and endangered architecture illustrated in this report.

GREAT BRITAIN'S NAVAL HERITAGE

by Jonathan Coad

From the time of the Tudor monarchs the Royal navy has played a key role in our national affairs. From small beginnings, confined largely to the North Sea and English Channel, it grew and evolved to meet the demands of trade and empire, becoming one of the largest navies the world had seen. If sea battles are the stuff of history and legend, no less important was the Royal Navy's role in the imposition and maintenance of the *Pax Britannica*. Freeing the high seas of pirates and making the trade routes safe have had incalculable effects on the growth of western civilisation.

None of the naval exploits would have been possible without the Royal Dockyards which were created to build and maintain the fleet. Alongside them were established associated facilities - ordnance depots, power magazines, victualling yards and naval hospitals. From the early eighteenth century onwards, similar, if more modest, facilities were created overseas.

Throughout the eighteenth century, the fleet grew both in overall numbers and in the size of individual warships. The extent of the sailing navy was to peak during the Napoleonic wars at just over 900 vessels, but by the 1750s government investment in the fleet and its shore facilities was such that it has been claimed with some justification that the Royal Navy was the greatest industrial power in the western world.

Until the mid nineteenth century, warships were timber built, wind powered and relied for their armament on massive broadsides of smooth-bore guns firing solid shot. By the 1850's, the Royal Navy was using steam power, but it was the introduction of the all-metal, armour-plated warship in 1860 which signalled the death of the wooden hulled fleet. By 1870, rifled muzzle-loading guns in armoured turrets were being introduced, masts, yards and sails were being abandoned and warships were assuming the appearance they were to keep until missiles replaced big guns and air-power made battleships vulnerable and obsolete.

Hand in hand with these naval developments went successive modernisations and expansions of the navy's shore facilities. Huge sums were expended largely rebuilding the main fleet bases at Portsmouth and Plymouth between 1760 and circa 1800. In the mid-nineteenth century, to cope with new technology and new materials, the Admiralty closed the Thames yards and grafted what were essentially new dockyards for the steam navy onto Portsmouth, Devonport and Chatham.

Great Britain today has a small but unparalleled collection of historic warships representing the main naval developments over the last 450 years - Mary Rose, HMS Victory, Foudroyant, Warrior, Gannet, Alliance and HMS Belfast. Less well known, but a no less vital element of our maritime heritage are the royal dockyards; without the latter a Royal Navy would hardly have been possible and our modern history would have been very different.

Today, the fleet operates from only two of the old dockyards - Portsmouth and Devonport - and from Rosyth, a creation of the early 20th century. Since 1950, dockyards at Singapore, Malta, Gibraltar, Bermuda, Sheerness and Chatham have been closed and in some cases extensively redeveloped. Little too remains of the unique mid-nineteenth century Haslar Gunboat Yard.

Nevertheless, there still exist representative examples of all the main types of naval buildings and engineering works, while the older part of Chatham Dockyard is now unique in being the only Georgian dockyard to survive almost intact. This statement though must not lull us into a false sense of security: we do have an exceptional heritage of naval buildings, the envy of other maritime countries, but their future is by no means secure.

The Royal Dockyards were essentially huge industrial complexes. Central to their existence - hence their name - were the dry-docks; grouped around these were the workshops and storehouses.

Elsewhere within the boundaries were houses for the senior dockyard officers, porters and watchmen.

Later, chapels were to be added. At Portsmouth, a Naval Academy, forerunner of Dartmouth, was built in the early 1730's; ninety years later the same dockyard saw construction of the first ever apprentice school for shipwrights.

The great rebuilding of Portsmouth and Devonport in the latter part of the eighteenth century means that few buildings in these yards predate 1760. By contrast, Chatham, which was far less systematically redeveloped, has buildings from every decade between 1700 and 1850. What remains of Sheerness is largely the work of Rennie at the end of the Napoleonic wars. Isolated naval buildings and engineering works still survive at the former dockyards at Harwich, Deptford, Woolwich and Pembroke, but the layouts, and hence much of the interest of these yards, have been totally lost.

It is difficult to write about Georgian naval architecture without giving undue prominence to Chatham. This dockyard is an extraordinary survival. Denied wholesale modernisation in the eighteenth century, largely bypassed by the creation of a new steam dockyard in the nineteenth century, and mercifully spared the bombing which so damaged Portsmouth and Devonport in the Second World War, Chatham has come down to us little altered from the age of Nelson and Trafalgar. Within its boundaries are virtually every type of naval building: the Commissioner's House of 1704, the Officers' Terrace of 1720, the Sail and Colour Loft of 1725, the earliest surviving naval storehouse ... the list is a lengthy one.

Highlights on it must be the great timber-framed Mast House and Mould Loft of 1753, almost certainly where HMS Victory's lines were laid out, and the great ropery complex rebuilt in the 1780s but incorporating buildings going back to the 1720s. Georgian and Victorian machinery remained in use here until naval ropemaking ceased at the end of 1982.

Brunel's Sawmill, Chatham Dockyard

From early in the 19th century is the great smithery, in use until 1976 and still containing much of its nineteenth century tools and equipment. Nearby stand the five enormous slip roofs built to protect wooden warships during their construction. The earliest is timber and dates from 1838, the next three are all-metal built in the mid 1840s while the range is completed by G T Greene's 7 Slip of 1852. This is now a unique group, the timber slip roof one of only three surviving in the country (the other two are at Devonport). Advanced technology here is represented by the Brunel steam sawmills of 1814 (the surviving machinery is not original) and Holl's fireproof Lead and Paint Mills of a few years later. Amidst all these wonders are the humbler dockyard buildings such as timber seasoning sheds, architecturally modest but important components of a Georgian dockyard.

The Ropery, Chatham

Slip Roof, Chatham

Portsmouth, by contrast, still exhibits much of its formal replanning of the 1760s. Then, the Navy Board and the dockyard officers made a sustained attempt to design an efficient, functional dockyard, grouping storehouses in one area, workshops in another, and bringing together the principal officers into one office building in the centre of the dockyard. From here, they overlooked the great complex of eighteenth century dry-docks, a group today without parallel in Europe. Just north of these stands the Block Mills, erected late in the eighteenth century to house the navy's first steam engine, but famous as the home of Marc Brunel's block-making machinery, a world 'first' in its use of machine tools for mass-production. His original machinery survives in Portsmouth, with other sets in the Science Museum and the Smithsonian.

Wartime bombing at Devonport all but obliterated the eighteenth century dockyard (South Yard), although individual buildings and the ghost of its layout remain. Fortunately, bombing largely spared Devonport's mid-nineteenth century contribution to naval architecture, the huge Quadrangle Factory in North Yard. This, designed by E M Barry, was built as a combination of foundry, machine and boiler shops, storehouses and workshops, to service the new steam navy. Building on the pioneer work of the now-vanished steam workshops at Woolwich, the Devonport Quadrangle is the supreme example of Victorian dockyard architecture. Its scale and internal flexibility behind its elaborate stone exterior has meant that it remains today very much at the head of modern Devonport.

Probably the first to establish facilities alongside the dockyards was the Board of Ordnance. Although the Board's gun manufacturing operations were centred at Woolwich (where the Arsenal has suffered years of shameful attrition and neglect), it remained primarily a purchasing department whose need was for dedicated storage facilities adjacent to the fleet bases.

Since the Second World War there have been two major losses of historic ordnance facilities: the Ordnance buildings adjacent to Chatham Dockyard demolished in the 1950s (before their historic worth was appreciated) and the great 1770 group of powder magazines at Purfleet (largely destroyed in the early 1970s after their importance had been pointed out).

Fortunately, there are still representative examples of Board of Ordnance work. Pride of place must go to Morice Yard, Devonport. This is an intact Ordnance yard laid out in the 1720s adjacent to the new Plymouth Dockyard. It still has its two original storehouses, their interiors largely unaltered, its terrace housing for the Ordnance officers, its porters' lodges and its powder magazine of some twenty years later. Sandwiched between the old dockyard (South Yard) and its Victorian sister (North Yard), by some miracle it largely escaped wartime damage and today remains very much in naval use.

The last twenty-five years have not been kind to naval ordnance property. The series of powder magazines at Marchwood, on Southampton Water, built during the Napoleonic Wars, were abandoned in the 1960s. Neglect and vandalism have taken their toll. At Tipner, on the eastern side of Portsmouth Harbour, the early nineteenth century naval powder magazines stand in increasing dereliction in the centre of a scrap yard. Listing here and scheduling of Marchwood have been shown to be ineffective in themselves in securing the future of these structures.

Losses at Purfleet, Marchwood and Tipner may be forgiven provided sensible and sensitive solutions are found for the ordnance complex at Priddy's Hard, Gosport. Laid out as a powder depot in the 1770s in a northern extension of the Gosport Lines, this still retains many of its original buildings, from the great powder magazine to the tiny camber quay and the ordnance storekeeper's house. Other buildings and a second powder magazine were added in the nineteenth century.

Priddy's Hard supplied both the fleet at Portsmouth and the massive Portsmouth and Gosport defences with ammunition. The depot for the weapons - the guns, side arms, muskets, cutlasses etc - lay adjacent to the dockyard at Gun Wharf, now HMS Vernon. Here remain a number of Board of Ordnance storehouses and offices from the late eighteenth and early nineteenth century. Architecturally, the most notable of these is the former Grand Storehouse erected late in the Napoleonic Wars. A well proportioned, pedimented brick building which unfortunately lost one of its wings in wartime bombing, it now stands derelict but perfectly capable of sympathetic re-use given the will and the means.

Feeding the fleet produced a naval catering industry well established a century and a half before the emergence on a comparable scale of any commercial rivals. Apart from a few surviving buildings from the old Royal Victoria Victualling Yard at Deptford, which were successfully converted to residential use by the GLC in the late 1960s, only two other historically important naval victualling yards remain in the UK. These are the Royal Clarence Yard at Gosport and the Royal William Yard at Stonehouse. The latter was laid out on a new site in the 1820s to a design by Rennie. The former was extensively rebuilt and extended during the same period to a design by G L Taylor, Navy Board Architect.

The Victoria, Clarence and William Yards were not just repositories for naval victuals, they were also manufacturing yards, in their heyday vast food-processing factories, established generations before commercial food factories of a similar size were built. At all three yards, beef and pig arrived on the hoof or by boat, were slaughtered, salted and packed in salt in barrels made in the yards elsewhere. Nearby, vast mill/bakeries received wheat, milled it, mixed and baked it into ships' biscuits, while elsewhere in the yards breweries maintained continuous production to slake naval thirsts.

At Clarence Yard, Gosport, stands a complete set of mid-eighteenth century cooperage buildings grouped round Cooperage Green. These remained in use until the ending of the naval rum ration in 1970. North of Cooperage Green, Taylor grafted on his new victualling yard. Wartime bombing has destroyed the brewery and one wing of the mill/bakery, but sufficient of the latter remains, including its original circular ovens, to form an impressive landmark on the Gosport waterfront. Behind it stand the houses of the victualling officers and the ranks of stalls for the cattle. Clarence Yard is still used by the navy, but its principal historic buildings now stand empty.

Unquestionably, the grandest of the victualling yards, one of the most remarkable examples of early nineteenth century planned layout of industrial buildings in the country, is the monumental Royal William Yard at Stonehouse, Plymouth. Rennie's original buildings and layout are still intact and the few later additions have been sympathetic in scale and design. Only Scamp's mid-nineteenth century naval bakery and flour mill in Malta comes anywhere near the grandeur of this great west country victualling base. Ideally situated across the Hamoaze from Devonport Dockyard, its limestone and granite buildings of sufficient size to cope with most modern methods of storage, the complex is now at risk following a Ministry of Defence decision to close the Royal William Yard in 1992, in the process running down essential maintenance.

Naval hospitals are another group of buildings once found adjacent to all the main fleet bases. By the middle of the eighteenth century, the Admiralty had come to accept that it had a responsibility for the proper care of its sick and wounded seamen. In part, this was due to pressure from a distinguished group of naval surgeons, in part it was the realisation that the existing contractor system, using a variety of rented accommodation, inns and ale-houses, was inefficient and expensive. With the navy venturing further afield as a matter of course by the beginning of the 18th century, mortality rates on the longer voyages mounted steeply. The capture of Gibraltar in 1704 and Minorca four years later, led to the construction of the first naval hospitals at these bases. Early hospitals still remain; that at Port Mahon was to be extensively rebuilt in the 1770s and now stands ruinous. Gibraltar hospital has been carefully converted to naval married quarters.

Gibraltar and Port Mahon hospitals, although purpose-built by the navy, initially were run by contractors. Until the 1740s, sailors landed in England sick or wounded continued to be cared for in a variety of contractor-run buildings. However, the outbreak of war in 1739 led to the virtual collapse of this system, overwhelmed by the sheer numbers needing aid. In 1745, the navy authorised construction of Haslar Hospital on the Gosport peninsula. This was to be run by the navy and was completed in 1761. It remains today the centre of naval medicine.

Haslar's design, which apparently owes much to the involvement of Theodore Jacobson, architect of the Foundling Hospital in London, by the 1780s catered for some 2100 patients, grouped in 84 wards. These wards ran the full width of the buildings, doubling as corridors and making medical isolation difficult. This situation was avoided at the navy's second hospital, begun at Stonehouse, outside Plymouth, in 1754. The architect was Alexander Rovehead who chose to group his wards in ten three-storey blocks, formally arranged round a courtyard and focussed on an administrative building and chapel in the centre of the main axis. Medically, this layout was a great advance on Haslar. Part of Stonehouse hospital suffered war damage, but the majority of Rovehead's buildings remain, as does his formal layout. Internally, one or two of the blocks still contain their nineteenth century stoves and fittings. Stonehouse Hospital may close shortly; its future must be a cause for concern.

Later, other naval hospitals were to be built at Great Yarmouth and at Chatham. The hospital at Great Yarmouth, built to cope with possible casualties from the Eastern Squadron during the Napoleonic wars, remains largely intact and is a local authority home. Chatham Hospital was demolished after the Second World War.

What of the future of this remarkable legacy of naval architecture? The bulk of the buildings and the engineering works such as dry-docks and slips in the active naval bases and in the former dockyard at Chatham are scheduled ancient monuments. Elsewhere, particularly at Sheerness, many of the buildings are listed. Such protection, though valuable, is no guarantee of immortality. Indeed, it can work against a building's survival if the owner assumes (wrongly) that such legal protection precludes any alterations or change of use.

At present, historic naval buildings divide themselves into four groups: those still in active naval bases; those for which MoD (N) has no use and wishes to dispose of; those which have passed into commercial hands and, finally, those in the care of preservation trusts.

The cost of maintaining an historic building owned by a government department rests with that department, whose first priority is not usually the proper care of historic fabric. The Royal Navy quite properly sees its role in life as the maintenance of an efficient modern fleet backed by efficient modern shore facilities. A budget-holding admiral, with limited funds, faced with paying maintenance on an empty historic building or on modern facilities for his sailors will, not unnaturally, usually choose the latter. As always, the secret of success is to try to ensure that historic buildings have viable and sympathetic modern uses and never stand empty.

A small number of buildings still in naval ownership are of such historic significance that, if appropriate naval uses cannot be found for them, they should be put in secure hands, preferably with sufficient funding or at a price which allows this. A notable example of this category of building is Brunel's Blockmills at Portsmouth.

Most naval buildings are quite capable of sympathetic adaption. Barry's Quadrangle at Devonport is in the midst of a huge modernisation programme which will adapt it for the 21st century navy without impairing its nineteenth century architectural qualities. A more modest scheme is being prepared for the old 1790 smithery in Portsmouth Naval Base. Recently, the Officers' Terrace at Portsmouth had six of its early eighteenth century houses converted into offices. The principal internal alterations involved cutting through the party walls on each floor to form spine corridors. Considerable care was taken to reduce alterations to the historic fabric to the absolute minimum. Strip lighting was avoided because of its disastrous appearance when viewed from outside, while fittings such as new doors were designed to be sympathetic to their historic surroundings. As a result, the terrace, including its rear ranges, has gained a new lease of life.

Such conversions are nothing new in dockyard history - eighteenth century naval records frequently mention adaptions and changes of use of dockyard buildings. These examples show that it is quite possible successfully to re-use naval buildings - provided there is vision and a will.

Where the Navy has no further use for groups of historic buildings and wishes to dispose of its estate, the needs of conservation should play their part in disposal plans. While in naval ownership, the buildings should continue to be maintained to ensure that historic fabric does not deteriorate. Safeguards should be agreed with local planning authorities to ensure that not just the buildings, but in many cases their settings, are preserved (see Priddy's Hard, below). Where there is a need for expensive repairs, perhaps due to the age of the buildings rather than to a lack of maintenance, the selling price should reflect this. If the buildings are to pass to a Preservation

Trust, they should come with a sufficient endowment to put buildings and their infrastructure into good order. It should not be the job of English Heritage (unless its funds are specifically augmented) or of other grant-giving bodies to make good the results of the Government's neglect of its own historic buildings.

There are currently three important groups of naval buildings in various stages of disposal. These are Royal William Victualling Yard, recently handed over to a Trust, Priddy's Hard at Gosport and, possibly, Stonehouse Hospital at Plymouth.

The Victualling Yard and Stonehouse Hospital are formal architectural compositions whose harmony depends as much on the maintenance of their layouts and settings as on the individual buildings. In both cases, the best hope for preserving not just the buildings but the equally important atmospheres of these famous naval establishments, lies in each being in the control of a single authority.

Royal William Yard's buildings are essentially industrial. Light engineering, storage, commercial offices are all possible uses which could easily be accommodated here with minimal adaption of historic fabric. Great care would be needed to control vehicle parking so that the main vistas remain uncluttered and strict controls would be needed to avoid a proliferation of commercial signs. If these conditions were met, Royal William Yard could have a viable future as well as being a tourist attraction.

A more exciting possibility would be to use Royal William Yard as the new University of Plymouth. At present, this is scattered round the city in the buildings of the old Polytechnic. Converted with imagination and sensitivity, this would give Plymouth one of the finest of all university campuses. It could also be the saving of the naval hospital if this is closed. Only a short distance away, the blocks of wards would lend themselves to conversion to students' halls of residence.

At Gosport, Priddy's Hard presents different problems. The 1770 Powder Magazine complex is of sufficient quality and rarity to be a visitor attraction in its own right, along with the projecting length of the Gosport Lines and the nearby mid-nineteenth century shell-filling rooms. Other ordnance buildings could find alternative commercial uses. Because this area remained an ordnance depot until very recently, the bastionned lines have not been encroached on as has happened elsewhere. There is thus a rare opportunity to preserve the setting of Priddy's Hard and its defences.

However, this will not happen if all the land outside the lines is sold for housing. If this occurs, the setting of this remarkable group could be seriously impaired and it will be more difficult for visitors to gain an appreciation of the defence function of the Lines. What is needed here is a bit of imagination and generosity. Part of the land outside and away from the Lines could be developed, but land adjacent to the ramparts should become parkland. Gosport is short enough of green spaces as it is. Priddy's Hard, its buildings now fast deteriorating, should be given to a body prepared to open it to visitors. Along with this should go an endowment based on the cost of bringing this important historic enclave to a good state of repair.

The preservation of complete dockyards and opening them to visitors began in the 1950s at the former Royal Navy dockyard at Antigua in the West Indies. This pioneer project was followed in the late 1970s at Bermuda, where the naval base had closed in 1951. On both islands, largely volunteer Trusts have achieved very considerable success. They are however helped by the small size of the dockyards (compared to the home bases) and by their geographical location. Cruise ships, yachts and tourists provide a steady flow of visitors, while careful conversion of some of the naval buildings at Antigua into holiday flats provides further income.

In England, one of the great success stories in conservation in the 1980s has to be the creation of the Chatham Historic Dockyard Trust with its government endowment and brief to preserve and find sympathetic uses for the old Georgian Dockyard. (Contrast this with the approach of English Estates who have systematically demolished most of the adjacent Victorian dockyard buildings).

The Chatham Trust faces a daunting task. A combination of inadequate funding and a tremendous backlog of repairs has stretched resources, despite extra aid from English Heritage. Nevertheless, much has been achieved: the ropery still makes ropes, the flag-loft still makes flags. Exciting exhibitions have been opened and sympathetic uses have been found for many of the buildings. The dry-docks are used both commercially and by historic vessels. Chatham, where both Georgian dockyard and its bastionned defences survive largely intact, should become one of Europe's major historic attractions. The creation of the Chatham Trust was followed by the establishment of a similar one to look after part of the historic core of Portsmouth Dockyard. Here the task is helped enormously by the existence of the Mary Rose, Victory and Warrior, together with the Royal Naval Museum. The buildings themselves are in basically sound condition and the Trust better endowed than Chatham. The task is more to provide visitor facilities for the existing crowds than to entice them in the first place.

Setting aside the ever-present financial constraints, what potential pitfalls are there for trusts which have charge of historic naval establishments? For visitors to gain a fuller appreciation of these remarkable enclaves, it is not just a question of preserving the physical evidence in the form of the buildings and engineering works: it is all too easy to damage or destroy the fragile atmosphere of these places. Naval architecture is a mixture, at its best robust and functional, focussed on the serious business of serving the fleet. Preservation of this purposeful feel is as important as preserving the buildings; here, minor details matter. At one end of the spectrum, ill-considered signs, a rash of bunting, troupes of entertainers masquerading as Jolly Jack Tars, the flotsam and jetsam of the Heritage Industry, can usually only detract. At the other, a sea of Heritage Good Taste, epitomised by the sudden appearance of acres of York Stone paving, cannon-shaped bollards and reproduction gas lamps can be equally inimical. Dockyards especially were working places where money for maintenance was often short. Tar stains, tarmac, oily water, fading paintwork, piles of lumber, good old fashioned dirt, grass in corners, a trace of dereliction, were part and parcel of the scene; if these are all sanitised away, we are left with chocolate-box dockyards such as never existed.

Enormous care also needs to be taken when introducing any new buildings. Indeed, there should be a presumption against so doing. At Chatham, the first phase of a new housing scheme has been largely tucked away behind other buildings. The second phase, if built, will dominate the northern end of the historic dockyard, altering its character for ever.

Where naval buildings are looked after by preservation trusts, normal criteria for judging the architectural worth of buildings need to be largely suspended. Dockyards are an amalgam of good, bad and indifferent architecture where it is the totality which is often so important. The huge pre-war 4 Boathouse at Portsmouth may dominate its eighteenth and nineteenth surroundings, but it is far more a part of dockyard history than any modern building which might replace it. Heritage in such a context ought to be about finding new uses for all buildings.

Where new buildings are needed in the historic settings of dockyards, high quality of design and materials should be used. The late twentieth century contribution to the dockyard scene should match the best of its Victorian and Georgian predecessors. The recent development of 'design and build' schemes inspires little confidence that naval bases will see new buildings of real quality; architecture of the trading estate and the business park is entering the royal dockyards. In the 1970s the navy commissioned a series of architecturally outstanding engineering workshops at Portsmouth and the great frigate complex at Devonport. More recently, it has been the historic trusts who have appreciated that good modern architecture is usually the best way to complement existing buildings.

Above: Stonehouse Naval Hospital, Plymouth Below: Royal William Victualling Yard, Plymouth

THE RANGE OF POST MEDIEVAL MILITARY BUILDINGS AND DEFENSIVE STRUCTURES

by Andrew Saunders

The extent and range of eighteenth and nineteenth century military buildings in Great Britain are predominantly influenced by the response to spasmodic invasion threats and fear of coastal raids on naval dockyards and commercial ports. Exceptions to the pre-occupation with coastal defence are the defensible barracks and military roads controlling the Highlands following the Jacobite Risings. Political opposition to the creation of a standing army meant that purpose-built barracks outside existing fortifications and military and naval towns like Berwick upon Tweed or Portsmouth were few. It was not until the war with Revolutionary France that barracks began to be built in order to accommodate a greatly increased army on a regular basis, and also as a precaution against revolutionary activities in the new manufacturing towns, followed by the military establishments at Woolwich, Camberley and Aldershot.

There was a strong element of geographical continuity in the concentrations of coastal defences during the eighteenth and nineteenth centuries which broadly reflected the priorities established in Henry VIII's reign when the main fleet anchorages were protected. First and foremost were the main naval bases of Portsmouth, Plymouth/Devonport, Chatham and Sheerness, and the Thames approaches to London commanded by Tilbury Fort. The defensive nucleus for each of these locations had been established during the reign of Charles II.

In addition there were the strategic ports such as Dover, Harwich, Hull and Tynemouth on the east coast. On the west, were the Fal estuary, Milford Haven, the Mersey and at Dumbarton on the Clyde. Towards the end of the nineteenth century, the main commercial ports, shipyards and munitions centres such as Aberdeen, Dundee, the Firth of Forth, Newcastle upon Tyne, and the Humber, as well as important naval anchorages, were given additional protection.

Ever since the Spanish Armada crisis, the likely invasion beaches had received attention though not on a substantial scale. The measures taken to deal with the Napoleonic danger in 1803-05 are typified by the distribution of Martello towers along the coasts of Kent and Sussex and of Essex and Suffolk. Other towers appeared in Orkney such as Crockness (below) to protect the convoy assembly point in Longhope Sound against commerce raiders.

Elsewhere, there are small but important concentrations of fortifications, in particular geographical localities such as the Isles of Scilly and the Isle of Wight, part of the wider defensive strategy for the Solent.

In Scotland conditions were different. As well as the Highland garrisons in defensible barracks, the traditional military centres of Edinburgh and Stirling Castles were maintained and improved. In addition to Highland garrisons was Fort George, built during the 1750s at Ardesier near Inverness.

During the eighteenth and first half of the nineteenth century, the forts and batteries at these defended locations followed a fairly consistent design pattern. The more permanent forts were enclosed by ditches and earth ramparts revetted in brick or stone. All, to one degree or another, were influenced by the conventions of the bastion system of fortification which had evolved in early sixteenth century Italy and reached its apogee in the works of Vauban in France and the Low Countries by the end of the seventeenth century. In essence, this had come to be a defensive system which demanded continuous lines, defence in depth and totality of flanking cover. Theory nevertheless always had to be subordinated to topography. The bastion system remained fundamentally unchanged for three hundred and more years because there were no far-reaching technological improvements to the weapons of the time, dependent as they were on black powder and smooth bore guns. One of the best preserved examples of the bastion system is Fort Tilbury in Essex, illustrated below.

Revolutionary technological changes occurred in the 1850s with the arrival of steam driven, armoured warships on the one hand, and the appearance of the rifled gun on the other, which dramatically extended both the range and accuracy of artillery. These developments radically altered the design of fortifications during the 1860's, requiring thicker masonry, greater use of earthwork, and guns mounted in bombproof casements protected by iron shields.

Advance in weapons technology came at an ever increasing pace throughout the rest of the nineteenth century. The greater efficiency of the rifled gun was complemented by more effective propellants and more destructive explosive projectiles. The quick-firing gun was developed, together with a new dimension in harbours and estuaries represented by the torpedo and the mine. All this brought a corresponding change in the defensive response, which either went to the extreme of thicker armour and underground works, or to a cheaper move towards simple earthworks and trenches made feasible by the defensive machine gun, combined with increasing mobility of gun batteries. British military thinking favoured the latter course.

The defence works of eighteenth and nineteenth century Britain can be structurally divided into six main types: forts, batteries, towers, defence lines (including fortified towns and dockyards), and harbour defences.

Forts were self-contained with provision for a permanent garrison enclosed within a well defined self-defensive system. The enclosing defences were essentially formed of rampart and ditch, sometimes duplicated with elaborate outworks, whose front was covered by flanking fire from bastions. During the course of the nineteenth century, bastions were superceded by various forms of ditch defence provided by projecting caponiers or by means of galleries in the masonry scarp or ditch counterscarp and continuous lines by rings of detached forts. The main armament might be mounted in open batteries on the rampart or in casemates behind the scarp walls.

Internally, arranged round a central parade, might be the 'domestic' buildings - officers and soldiers barracks, Governor's House, Master Gunner's House, chapel, sutler's house (where provisions were for sale), magazines, artillery stores, hospital, gatehouse, guardroom and cells, stables, artillery/small arms stores, waggon sheds, ball court etc.

Batteries were much simpler. They might be a sequence of open gun platforms behind an earth parapet or they could be enclosed by a wall to the rear, with minimal self defence, and with associated buildings limited to a guard house and a magazine.

Gun towers are not limited to the familiar Martello type either in date or form. They may have an attendant battery. They usually could accommodate a small garrison.

Defence lines may vary from the continuous bastioned enclosure of a town, to the trenches of fieldworks protecting an encampment or a series of detached redoubts to a landscape feature such as the Royal Military Canal in Kent. By the mid-nineteenth century rings of detached forts well outside the dockyard had superceded the traditional continuous bastioned trace.

Harbour defences are more applicable to the late nineteenth century armaments expansion incorporating novel weapons: controlled minefield, defence lights (searchlights), and guided torpedo stations.

Beyond the limits of these various forms of fortification was provision for the regimental soldier. His accommodation during much of the eighteenth century was greatly influenced by political objections to the creation of a standing army and for long it was based on taverns. Outside the long established garrisons in medieval castles and coastal forts there were few military buildings in the eighteenth century. Individual barrack buildings were rare apart from those with policing connotations in the Highlands and Ireland.

Change came after 1792 with the re-organisation of the army pushed through by William Pitt soon after the start of the Revolutionary Wars with France. A military department was created, not only without Parliamentary sanction, but independent thereof. This was the Barrack Master General's Office. In 1792, there was only sufficient barrack accommodation for 20,000 men. Fifteen years later, there were 203 barracks for 17,000 cavalry and 146,000 infantry. Part of their purpose was to police the growing manufacturing towns. With various army reforms of the nineteenth century, more barracks were established in county towns and the larger industrial centres. These were later amplified by the effects of the developing 'volunteer' and then the Territorial movements which required different forms of structures such as drill halls.

Above: Nineteenth century Barracks at Devizes

The need to improve conditions for the garrisons was recognised with the improvement of barrack buildings, leading to the introduction of such features as school rooms and regimental institutes.

Other military buildings besides barracks outside the confines of a fortress or immediately related to a coastal defence work, were the major magazines at Purfleet, Priddy's Hard etc and the Powder Mills at Waltham Abbey, Faversham etc. Weapon manufacturing is represented by such establishments at Woolwich Arsenal and the Armstrong works at Elswick. Training was effected at Woolwich (Royal Military Academy) and in the Camberley/Aldershot complex. All these establishments present a wide range of specialised structures. There are also military hospitals, prisons, schools and stores.

With the turn of the twentieth century, warfare took on far wider dimensions with the invention of the aeroplane and the airship, more effective submarines, and, during the First World War, the arrival of the armoured vehicle on the battlefield. By 1939, the concept of 'blitzkrieg' and total war on civilians made it necessary for extraordinary defensive measures and defence works to become nationwide for the first time. Airfields proliferated, each one with its decoy site to divert the attention of hostile bombers. Anti-aircraft and searchlight batteries and the radar towers of an early warning system were extensive. The threat of 'Operation Sealion' in 1940 saw the construction of 'emergency batteries' around the coast and inland the creation of anti-tank ditches and stoplines of pillboxes across the countryside. All manner of strongpoints and obstacles to a German advance were prepared.

All these have had a profound and lasting effect upon the historic landscape. Many of the wartime structures were of a temporary nature and were in no condition to survive. Many have been deliberately swept away as eyesores without regard to possible historic interest. Fifty years after the event, the residual 'monuments' of the Second World War have become a source of serious study and discovery, their sites are being registered in the National Monuments Record by the Royal Commissions on Historical Monuments and a selected few scheduled and listed by the Department of National Heritage, and the Secretaries of State for Scotland and Wales.

Twentieth century defensive works are bewildering in their variety and extent. The airfield is the most complex of all. Early runways were simply grass but around it were hangers of great variety, some going back to 1914. Flight control buildings, weapons testing ranges, technical and store buildings proliferated. The airfield domestic buildings were designed in characteristic architectural styles whether barrack blocks, officers' mess, or guardroom. Around the perimeter may be defensive rings of pillboxes (including the idiosyncratic, elevating, Pickett Hamilton pillbox) and battle headquarters.

Anti-aircraft defences consist of clustered gun positions shielded by low concrete walls and linked to observation and gun control structures.

Preparations against invasion were undertaken in the space of three or more months in 1940. The beach defences of 'emergency batteries' with their battery control and searchlight positions have been most vulnerable to clearance campaigns. Inland, the stoplines of pillboxes of many types and anti-tank obstacles have a higher degree of survival.

There are relics of civil defence measures chiefly in the form of shelters, but features such as warden posts and gas decontamination centres can still be identified.

Early warning devices remain from the First World War and from the 1930s in the form of large concrete sound mirrors and elements of the early radar CH and CHL systems survive. The look-out posts of the Royal Observer Corps still exist as well as the control centre at Winchester.

The major command and control centres such as the Whitehall War Room and the Combined Services command centre at Dover Castle (illustrated below) are now available to the public.

Wartime structures began to be removed rapidly at the end of the war. In 1956 came the abolition of coastal defence and with it the first major disposals of military sites. This is a process which has continued ever since, together with an increasing reluctance on the part of the Ministry of Defence to maintain those statutorily protected historic structures for which it is responsible.

A small sample of the nationally most important fortifications are in the care of the main government preservation agencies (English Heritage and Historic Scotland) such as Dover Castle, the Western Heights and part of Fort George. The National Trust and a few local authorities, principally in Hampshire, have also sought to preserve such sites as have specially formed local building preservation trusts.

Outside the umbrella of bodies with primary responsibility for conservation are a number of defence works which are of national importance within the Ministerially accepted criteria - rarity, representative of a particular type, of historic significance, innovative as well as condition and state of survival. Some of these are still in military occupation, substantially complete and mostly unvandalised, such as Fort Burgoyne in Kent, Forts Monckton and Elson in Hampshire and Tregantle and Scraesson Fort in Cornwall.

Despite an official policy for selective preservation there have been serious losses which have diminished the stock of historic exemplars. Perhaps the most tragic was the destruction of Sheerness as a military entity. It was, apart from Berwick upon Tweed, the only English town to retain its complete bastioned enceinte. Even now the residual 17th century defences are increasingly mutilated by the development of the ferry terminal.

The Purfleet powder magazine establishment has been reduced to a single magazine building. The Chatham ring forts are seriously diminished as an entity and a particular loss are the Twydall Redoubts, Gillingham, which were seminally important in the course of British military engineering.

Then too, there are individual losses of crucially important forts and batteries including Fort Wallington, Hampshire, Fort Pitt and Grain Fort in Kent and the Spanish Battery at Tynemouth.

Substantial destruction has taken place at many of the 19th century forts around Milford Haven, Pembrokeshire as well as at Eastbourne Fort, Sussex, Picklecombe Fort and Cawsand Battery, Cornwall, Fort Fareham and Fort Victoria, Isle of Wight.

Twentieth century defence works are particularly vulnerable and have suffered proportionally worse than other categories because of their recent date, ignorance of their special features and general lack of visual appeal. Important losses to early aviation history include the Farnborough Balloon Shed of 1917 and Aircraft Shed 'G; at Calshot, built in 1916-17. The historic Battle of Britain airfield of Hawkinge, Kent, has largely been destroyed and this is true for many more airfields. RAF Biggin Hill, the most famous airfield in the country is gradually being sold off by the MoD.

Examples of the emergency batteries are now few due to the 'tidying up' of coastal 'eyesores' and often with government aid. Pill boxes and strongpoints and roadside features are also vulnerable with many losses. One characteristic feature of anti-invasion defences, the flame fougasse alongside roads, is probably now extinct.

In many cases forts and batteries are deteriorating through erosion and neglect, such as Cockham Wood Fort, Kent, Maker Redoubts, Cornwall and Paull Fort, Humberside. Spurn Point WW1 complex, Humberside is threatened by coastal erosion. Even forts in the care of English Heritage: Landguard Fort, Suffolk (20th century Darells Battery in particular) and Fort Cumberland are deteriorating through lack of attention.

There are, however, encouraging examples of new use and straightforward preservation: New Tavern Fort, Gravesend, has been acquired by a local voluntary trust as have Harwich Redoubt and Nothe Fort, Weymouth. The Surrey Historic Buildings Trust/Surrey County Council have restored Chatley Semaphore Tower, Cobham which is open to the public, and the Coalhouse Fort Project was set up to achieve similar aims at Tilbury.

The Landmark Trust includes fortifications among the properties it is prepared to repair to run as holiday accommodation, including West Blockhouse Battery, Milford Haven, Pembrokeshire and Crownhill Fort, Plymouth.

Above: The Chatley Semaphore Tower Below: Coalhouse Fort, East Tilbury

THE FORTRESS STUDY GROUP

and Artillery Forts in Great Britain

by Jock Hamilton-Baillie

In June 1974 a number of military historians and others interested in fortifications met at Pembroke College, Oxford, to consider what could be done to encourage the study and care of these works. They agreed that early medieval castles and older defences were already well covered, but that later works were not. They decided to found a small society to coordinate study and research into such works and to publish a journal on the subject; they chose the name "The Fortress Study Group"; a Chairman, Editor and Secretary were appointed. The first volume of their Journal, named "Fort", was published in the spring of 1975 and the first Conference was held at Southampton in September of that year.

The membership grew faster than had been anticipated and came from a much wider variety of interest. From the start, studies of fortifications have been world wide and the society has considered itself to be international. Between a quarter and a third of the members have come from outside the United Kingdom. The work of the Fortress Study Group as an advice centre and pressure group working for the preservation and restoration of surviving works has mostly been confined to this country, but they have established close relations with national societies in other countries with similar aims.

As the society got bigger, a formal Constitution was adopted. After much discussion the field of interest was defined as "all aspects of fortifications and their armaments, especially works constructed to mount or resist artillery". Most of their work has been in the latter field, but this still includes an enormous range of interest. From the introduction of firearms in the fourteenth century to the early sixteenth century, fortresses were provided with gunports, though they were still "castles" in the ordinary meaning of the word, rather than "forts". They clearly come within the remit of the Fortress Study Group. At the other end of the range are the batteries, pillboxes and other works built to defend this country in the Second World War as well as the massive lines overseas such as the Maginot, Westwall and Atlantic Wall.

The variety in between is huge, but here I will limit myself to surviving works in this country. An example at the early end is Cooling Castle in Kent, built from 1381 to 1385. At first sight it looks like every child's idea of a castle, to be defended with bows and arrows and boiling oil, but on a closer look it can be seen that all the numerous embrasures, except two in the outer gate, are gunports not arrow slits. It is in private ownership and well looked after, which shows it can be done! For the next century or more, residential castles were equipped with gunports, but as time went on, except in Scotland, more for status than for serious effect. The first big change is in Henry VIII's great coast defence scheme from the Thames to Cornwall, where the larger works are still called castles but look like forts. Most, though of great interest as purpose designed artillery forts, do not need lobbying by Fortress Study Group for their protection.

As Henry VIII's castles were being built, a new pattern was sweeping through Europe which was to dominate fortification for three hundred years. This was the angle bastion system. These bastions have two faces meeting at a point towards the enemy and two flanks, turned back to the line of the curtain wall, which give enfilade fire along the faces of the neighbouring bastions. Good early examples, both well looked after, are Carisbrook and, on a more massive scale, Berwick-on-Tweed. Vauban, Chief Engineer to Louis XIV, was the most famous exponent of this system but worked at about the mid point of its history.

The next use of fortification in this country was in the Civil War and took various forms, all in temporary construction. Nothing remains of the elaborate bastioned enceinte at Oxford or the less formal works at London. At Newark, however, many signs remain of both the defending Royalists and the attacking Parliament and Scots. Little has been done to preserve them, but recently some restoration has started, just in time, on the most important fort called the Queen's Sconce. Fortunately they were all very well recorded by the Royal Commission on Historic Monuments.

Many castles, by now quite obsolete as forts, were defended by Royalist owners; usually bastioned earthworks were hastily added, which could be held while the attacking artillery demolished the ancient walls. A lovely example of an earth sconce, a four bastioned fort, is in an open field by the drainage canals near Erith in the Fens. It has a 1940 home guard steel turret on one bastion!

Above: Twentieth century fortifications at Tynemouth Castle

This illustrates a recurring feature of defence works. A strategic position usually remains so, and its fortifications are repeatedly replaced, remodelled and up-gunned over long periods of time. Dover Castle is an extreme example, where the ditch of Iron Age origin was extended in 1940 by concrete anti-tank obstacles. It was a fortification throughout this period. Another example comes from the Restoration period. The Dutch, having disgraced us at Chatham, tried to do the same at Harwich. Their first move had to be the capture of Landguard Fort, at the end of the long spit that runs south from Felixstowe, and covers the entrance to the port of Harwich. Despite getting a large force ashore, supported by the guns of their fleet, they were, as it says on a marble plaque on the site, "utterly repulsed". The plaque is now among brambles on a 1940 battery, but behind it are much of the five bastioned brick fort built after the Dutch attack, the heavy Victorian batteries spliced onto that, a controlled minefield station and many heavy gun positions, the last operational until 1956.

As the only fort in England to have been seriously attacked and as a British success, it is a shame that it is not a show place. It is in the care of English Heritage, who try and keep the main structure weather and vandal proof. This illustrates a major problem. Works such as this are very large. To put them in good order and safe for visitors is very expensive and even then there remains a heavy permanent maintenance cost. Unless the site can pay its way to some extent, this may be prohibitive. At the same time, insensitive alterations to improve profitability may be quite unacceptable, especially at such a work as Landguard with its high historical and architectural importance.

Tilbury Fort was built in a Dutch style by De Gomme, chief engineer to Charles II and though re-armed regularly until the last war, has retained its very elegant original form. It is beautifully maintained by English Heritage and open to the public. It is a pity the modern flood defences had to go between it and the Thames, obscuring the riverside battery, which was its main raison d'etre. Another success story is Fort George at Inverness, built after the '45 rebellion. The handsome original barracks have been modernised without spoiling their appearance and the defences have been restored by Historic Scotland and remain open to the public; it is an excellent solution.

Coming to the period of the Napoleonic wars, the picture is not so good. Again the size of the works is an obstacle to their restoration. The largest of all was the Royal Military Canal, round the landward edge of Romney Marshes, a likely enemy landing place. Despite its name it was a defensive line with a large wet ditch and rampart, on a stepped trace giving a flanking position every 600 yards. The eastern end is defended by a large bastion and other works below Shorncliffe Camp and the line was - and is - continuous for 19 miles to the River Rother. Here there is a lock, as the ditch had a secondary role as a canal for the quick movement of troops against a landing. It continues for some miles further west of the Rother, back to the coast. At the time of writing, the most interesting length adjoining the eastern defences is under threat by developers who wish to destroy it to make a marina. It is a scheduled monument, but in an earlier application (that failed over a Parliamentary Bill), English Heritage did not defend it and consent was given without discussion.

Further along the coast, at the mouth of Langstone Harbour, an earlier earthen Fort Cumberland had, in the 1780s, been destroyed to build a larger masonry work. This progressed very slowly, but by 1815 was completed. It is a pentagonal bastioned fort with the proper outworks, all following the ideas of Vauban. The outworks survive, though very overgrown and the fort is complete apart from war damage. There is nothing like it in Great Britain; the nearest are the single front on the landward face of Fort George and the earlier style bastions of Tilbury, both described above. It is used by English Heritage as a depot, but is not restored or open to the public. It is said that English Heritage will soon move out. It would make a wonderful addition to the military heritage of Portsmouth and Hampshire if they could take it on.

The greater part of the bastioned enceintes of Portsmouth and Devonport have been filled in long ago, but much of that at Chatham has survived. In about 1805 the older earth ramparts were extended and revetted in brick. The defences at the southern end, including the older Amherst redoubt, become very elaborate, including underground works. This section, known as Fort Amherst, has been taken over by a local volunteer society who, with some support from the local authorities, are doing an excellent job of restoration. They raise money by entrance fees to the completed parts and by various functions and entertainments. Their progress is necessarily slow and they deserve all the support they can get. Much of the rest of the lines survives, though one length has been filled in recent times and most is overgrown. One hopes that in the fullness of time more will be restored.

After the defeat of Napoleon I there was a lull in the building of fortifications, but it revived in mid century for fear of Napoleon III. By now, at long last, the bastion trace had gone out of favour, to be replaced by individual "polygonal" forts. With the longer range of rifled guns these could cover the intervals between them, though where they existed, enceintes were retained as backstops. The main danger was now seen to be attacks on our dockyards and the Royal Commission of 1860 set out a grandiose plan for their fortification. This consisted of coastal batteries against direct attack and rings of landward facing forts to protect the naval bases from forces who had landed elsewhere. Some of the rings were never completed for lack of money and in others the work went very slowly, but many large polygonal forts were built. They have, rather unkindly, been called Palmerston's Follies, but the best forts deter attack and who can be certain that these did not do so; furthermore could Palmerston have foreseen that in 1870 the Germans would remove the threat from France?

Most of the forts remained in military occupation until modern times; in 1940 many were incorporated in local defence schemes and some mounted anti-aircraft batteries. At other times

Below: Fort Brockhurst, polygonal land fort of 1858, now in the care of English Heritage

they were used as barracks, depots and stores, rather than as forts. The fact that shortage of money slowed down the construction adds to the interest of the Chatham ring, as the development of ideas can be followed.

The second half of the nineteenth century was a time of very rapid development of artillery. At the start, guns looked much as they had done for a hundred years or more; those mounted at its end continued in service to the last of coast defence in 1956. This resulted in a great variety and much alteration of coastal batteries, that mounted ever larger guns in armoured casemates, in pits on disappearing mountings and finally in "barbette" mountings, firing over an open parapet. A special type were the round masonry and iron armoured towers in the sea approaches to the ports; they too started with muzzle loaders in casemates and mostly ended with modern guns in barbette on the roof. One of the biggest, No-Mans-Land in Spithead, was recently converted by a developer into a millionaire's residence. Most coastal batteries remained operational in both world wars thus helping to preserve their predecessors, Henrican, Napoleonic or Victorian.

The last land fort to be completed was Fort Darland in about 1900, finishing the Chatham ring. Sadly, soon after the Second World War, it was completely destroyed. In the First World War pillboxes appeared for the first time, looking very much like those of the Second, near the east coast. An interesting but vain project of the first war, was the mounting on land of two twin 12 inch turrets from an obsolete battleship, one each side of the mouth of the Tyne. The underground concrete structures needed to do this were huge and the guns were only test fired right at the end of the war. Soon afterwards they were scrapped. The southern emplacement has been destroyed by quarrying, but, at the northern, the concrete ring, where the turret turned, can still be seen in the grass; the gun-pit is filled in but it is believed that the underground chambers are all still there. Perhaps someone will investigate it one day.

In 1940 this country faced the most serious threat of invasion, certainly since that of Napoleon I and possibly since 1066. Numerous emergency batteries, mostly mounting ex-naval guns were added to the existing coastal batteries; beach obstacles of scaffolding etc were constructed which have all disappeared, as we hope have the beach mines. Beach exits were obstructed with concrete anti-tank blocks, many of which are still there and a great variety of pillboxes were built. These were not only near the shore but in several lines further back ending at the GHQ line which started on the Bristol channel, ran eastwards doubled on the Avon-Thames line and Avon-Kennet Canal line, then single from south of Reading to Aldershot, south of London (near a curious late Victorian defence line), north towards the Wash and on, well inland, and into Scotland, although much of this was never completed.

Pillboxes also defended all airfields and later selected "anti-tank islands" in the south. Something between 15,000 and 18,000 were at least started in the three months after Dunkirk, a colossal effort. The Fortress Study Group would like to see as many as possible preserved. At least the Royal Commission for Historic Monuments in England, and their opposite numbers in Scotland have decided that all war time sites including batteries, anti-aircraft sites, pillboxes etc, that still exist should be recorded. It is a very large task, but a start has been made by a sub-group of the Fortress Study Group, working for them.

The history of our heritage of fortifications since the Second World War has been sad. The emergency batteries were quickly scrapped and in 1956 it was decided that coast defence was no longer required. All guns were removed and destroyed. So thoroughly was this done that not even museum examples were kept. The Royal Engineers not so long ago managed to bring back a complete 9.2 inch gun from Gibraltar for the Imperial War Museum, who have mounted it, looking rather forlorn, on Duxford Airfield. A spare barrel went to the Royal Artillery Museum where it is on a proving carriage. The battery positions were mostly left to the vandals, scrap merchants, rust and decay, including very often the older and larger forts in which they had been sited. Kent County Council set up a "removal of eyesores" fund, which methodically destroyed batteries in their area, including those of the heavy guns that had engaged the Germans in and over the Channel. Since the war, the Ministry of Defence have over the years, disposed of most of the land forts, either by sale to private owners or by handing over to local authorities. Any gap in occupation resulted very quickly in massive damage by vandals. At Chatham, Woodlands is badly damaged, Horsted is in unsympathetic occupancy and Borstal, much the best preserved has now passed into private hands from the Prison Service and its future is in doubt. At Portsmouth things are rather better but Wallington, a large Palmerston fort, has been destroyed.

To finish on a happier note, I believe the tide has now turned. Local authorities are much more aware of the value of their military heritage, Hampshire County Council especially. A good number of forts are now in good hands. Most of the older works are well cared for by English Heritage and Historic Scotland and Cadw. Where modern works are on the same site as ancient ones, not long ago they were ignored in the guide books: Dover and Tynemouth Castles were examples, but now this is not so. Far more fortifications are scheduled or listed, including some pillboxes. The National Trust now look after forts on their land, notably Old Needles Battery. The Landmark Trust have four forts including the very large Crownhill at Plymouth, which, by the good co-operation of the City Council had no "vandals gap".

Then there are the forts taken over most gallantly by local volunteer societies. Among them are New Tavern Fort at Gravesend, the first and very successful Harwich Redoubt, the Nothe Fort in Weymouth, Fort Amherst, which has already been mentioned and Coalhouse on the Thames where they are having a difficult time and need all the support they can get.

Lastly there are forts in sympathetic individual ownership, Spitbank in Spithead is an example. So until recently was Fort Perch Rock on the Mersey but the owner has to give up and its future is now in doubt.

It would be nice to think that some of the improvement has been due to the work of the Fortress Study Group. It is not really for the author to say, but at least most of it has happened since their founding.

SCOTTISH DEFENSIBLE PLACES AND GUNPOWDER WEAPONS 1450-1900

by Iain MacIvor

The earliest recognisable Scottish provision for guns in defence appears from the middle years of the fifteenth century - substantially later than in England. There is an immediately apparent certainty and sophistication in what is probably the earliest work, a battered rectilinear wall with low round towers, pierced by "inverted key-hole" and "dumb-bell" loops at Threave Castle in the south-west. The loops and the inwardly splayed openings behind them were designed for the emplacement of built-up wrought iron breech-loading guns maybe of 65mm and 80mm bore, of the type later called serpentines. This armament traversed, rather crudely in the contemporary English and European manner, on long timber stocks.

There is nothing tentative about the Threave outer wall, and we must remember that there is evidence of gunpowder weapons in Scottish hands for seventy years before it was built; the early part of the story that we are able to piece together may very much depend on accidents of survival. Inverted key-hole loops also appear in the near-contemporary parts of Ravenscraig Castle (illustrated below) on the north shore of the firth of Forth, and there are more examples of both kinds of loops clustered around the end of the century. These gun-loop forms, at first seen only in the strongholds of magnates or royalty and clearly meant for serious use, were to become a leitmotif of secular Scottish architecture for the nobility and gentry well into the seventeenth century and it is often open to debate whether they were security systems, chic ornaments, or both. Then as a tailpiece they were fashionably revived, appearing as part of the vocabulary of Scottish Baronial.

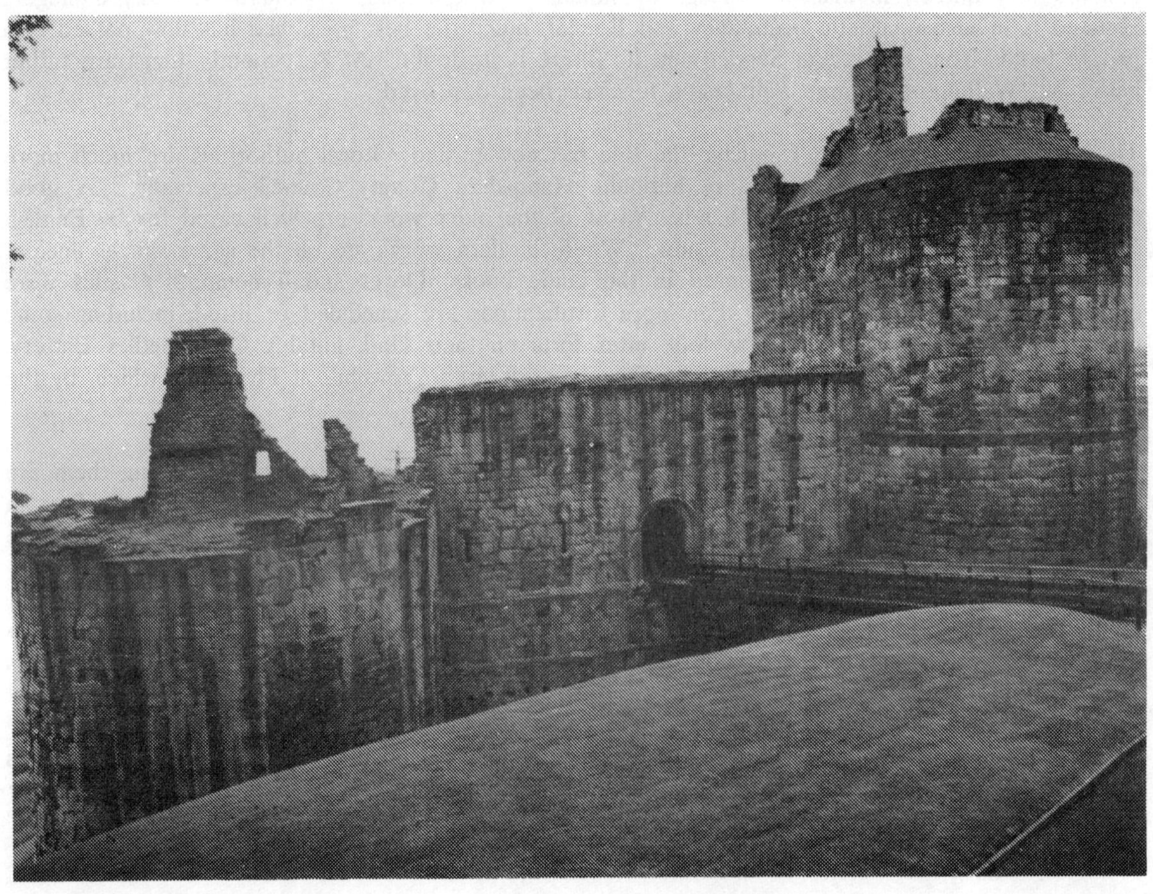

Similarly perpetuated and revived was the succeeding form of loop with a round throat splaying outward to a horizontal slit with rounded ends. The form seems to have been brought to Scotland from France by the master mason of John Stewart Duke of Albany, called from France to be Governor of Scotland just after the battle of Flodden. Albany established himself at Dunbar Castle, and between 1515 and 1523 built there a massive blockhouse advanced from the main front of the promontory castle and powerfully armed with French artillery: big guns on the parapet, lesser pieces firing through the loops below, emplaced in casemates within walls up to 6.5m thick. The squat blockhouse is shaped like an Italian angle-pointed bastion, though the resemblance is probably due rather to the form of the site than to conscious imitation of la nuova fortificazione. Even so, the Dunbar blockhouse is a most outstanding work of its age. Its thick walls and big loops, though not its forward-looking low profile, were imitated in the 1530s with the reinforcement of Tantallon and Blackness Castles.

That decade also saw the new building of the last private stronghold intended to have a major defensive capability, Sir James Hamilton of Finnart's Craignethan Castle in Clydesdale with it uniquely surviving caponier (illustrated above) and, among other features, an extraordinary double-pile residential tower.

While taking note of these masonry structures, we are reminded of the virtual disappearance of a whole category of defensive works in the story of the 1523 attack on the Border castle of Cessford, the seat of the Warden of the East Marches, by the Earl of Surrey. The English force was very respectably provided with three heavy siege guns as well as lesser pieces, but the earthworks around the place enabled the Warden's men to hold off the attempt. Today the strong ruined tower of Cessford is conspicuous, but the earthworks have almost disappeared and there is scarcely anything of near-contemporary earthwork elsewhere in Scotland, although it must have figured significantly in fortification.

The use of earthwork is however clearly evidenced in physical remains as well as documentary sources in the next development, the widespread introduction of the angle-pointed bastion by English and French armies in the course of their interventions into Scottish affairs between 1547 and 1560. Earthwork was substantially used both in free-standing forts and the fortification of towns - Leith by the French, Haddington by the English - and in most instances was faced with a masonry scarp. Today the extensive town defences have been destroyed, but the English and French promontory forts at Eyemouth and the English fort at Dunglass, on or near the Berwickshire coast, survive to show variants on the revolutionary new forms.

There are also French masonry remains at Inchkeith in the Forth and at Stirling Castle. In 1560, however, the end of direct French involvement and a degree of detente with England halted the expression of European mainstream ideas. During the long reign of James VI (1567-1625) ambiguous provision for light gunpowder weapons proliferated in secular building, while serious fortification stagnated. The most conspicuous extant work of the period is the Half Moon and Forewall at Edinburgh Castle as new built and remodelled after the devastating 1573 siege. The Half Moon certainly looks old fashioned even though it is possible to see it as an ingenious solution to awkwardness of site and pre-existing structures.

During the whole of the seventeenth century save for the period of the Commonwealth, although Scotland and England were ruled by the same king, they otherwise remained as entirely separate realms. In the reign of Charles I Scotland slid into civil war earlier than England. After a series of tortuous politico-ecclesiastical and military events, which produced a surviving temporary bastioned earthwork at Duns in Berwickshire, Oliver Cromwell invaded and occupied Scotland, the two states were forcibly joined as the United Commonwealth, and a series of formidable regular town defences and forts were built and garrisoned by the New Model Army. These included the first modern works in the Highlands: an outstanding bastioned pentagon just outside Inverness and a smaller earthwork fort in the remote and troublesome country of Lochaber. The mid-seventeenth century works there and in the Lowlands have been badly eroded by late developments. The Highland garrisons give a preview of future patterns of defence, though more immediately the Commonwealth's contribution was negated after the Restoration with the slighting of its works and now through Scotland only fragments survive. Charles II's Scottish government built a small fort in Shetland during the Dutch Wars to protect shipping in the Sound of Bressay, but actual achievement elsewhere was limited in spite of ambitious proposals for Edinburgh Castle.

James VII's displacement from the Scottish throne in favour of William and Mary in 1689 created a body of the disaffected, immediately named the Jacobites, especially strong in parts of the Highlands. As a security measure the United Commonwealth fort in Lochaber was reconstructed and renamed Fort William - in a bleak episode of Scottish history, a party set out from this fort to Glencoe in 1692. Disaffection increased with the Act of Union of 1707 which unified Scotland and England and led Louis XIV in the following year to attempt a sea-borne invasion of Scotland to put James VII's son back on the throne. The fleet turned back from the Forth but Queen Anne's government was alarmed by the ghost of the Franco-Scottish alliance and began hastily planned works at key strongholds. They were too hastily planned, as it turned out, for they had to be much modified and the hornwork planned for Edinburgh Castle abandoned. But they have left an important counterguard at Stirling Castle together with, at Edinburgh, the first purpose-designed garrison buildings in Scotland.

The next in a series of crises came with Anne's death and the Elector of Hanover's successor as George I. After the rising of 1715 was suppressed counter-measures were taken which mark the beginning of the best-known chapter in our story. In 1717 the Board of Ordnance (since the Act of Union, the body responsible for military works for the whole of Britain) planned four lightly fortified barracks with bastion-shaped towers for small arms defence in the Highlands. The most distant of these, at Bernera, commanding the principal sea crossing to Skye, had not long been completed when the Government, still very uneasy about disaffection and endemic lawlessness, sent Major-General George Wade to the north in 1724 to advise on measures to improve the situation.

Above: The abandoned barracks at Bernera, Skye

Below: The eighteenth century Governor's House, Edinburgh Castle

Wade, whose position was soon consolidated by his appointment as Commander-in-Chief in Scotland, had a profound influence in setting up a new military presence. A chain of strongpoints was established along the Great Glen, linking a new fort at Inverness Castle to a rebuilt Fort William, together with another new fort near the mid-point of the chain, the head of Loch Ness, replacing one of the 1717 barracks. The replacement was named Fort Augustus after George II's third son, William August, Duke of Cumberland, but the Roman echo is extremely apt. As in the Roman occupation of northern England and the Lowlands of Scotland, the chain of forts was connected by a military road, and Wade's soldiers also constructed roads replacing traditional tracks south from the Great Glen chain towards the "legionary fortress" at Edinburgh. The parallel was seen at the time. The magnificent Tay Bridge at Aberfeldy carrying the road to Fort Augustus, built by William Adam as Master Mason to the Board of Ordnance, bears a latin inscription referring to the road stretching north from the Roman frontier (of the Antonine Wall), and giving Wade the title of propraetor.

In the Lowlands, during Wade's term of office the engineer for North Britain, John Romer, improved the defences of Edinburgh and Dumbarton Castles - from the latter the next military road, to Inverary, was begun soon after Wade had moved on from his Scottish command - with works of middling strength that are today striking features of both places. At both, too, a very comely contemporary Governor's house survives.

In the 1745-46 rising misfortune overtook several of the recent works. The three barracks of the 1717 programme were taken and burnt, Ruthven in Badenoch having successfully resisted the first Jacobite attack. The fort at Inverness Castle and Fort Augustus were besieged, taken and blown up by Prince Charles Edward's army in the last stages of the rising, while Edinburgh and Stirling Castles and Fort William held off varying degrees of investment.

The eventual defeat of the Jacobites at Culloden left George II's government with a worrying recognition that it might happen again with a different outcome. At the same time it was accepted that Wade's overall plan of Highland forts linked to each other and to the south by improved land communications had been sound, even though the required strength of the forts had been under-estimated. After a false start when it was proposed to reconstruct the Cromwellian citadel at Inverness, it was decided to keep Forts Augustus and William much as they had been, while concentrating on an entirely new design by the engineer William Skinner for an impregnable base on a peninsula jutting out into the Moray Firth east of Inverness.

Fort George

The new stronghold, to be called Fort George, was in 1748. In addition the network of military roads was to be greatly extended with two ancient Aberdeenshire castles remodelled as small defensible barracks on the line of the road to Fort George.

The latter survives as an example of military engineering which is marvelled at by all its visitors. The shape of the peninsula guided a design with its main defences concentrated on one front towards the east, with a large ravelin and bastions, a broad ditch that could be filled with sea water by sluices, and a covered way with traverses and lunettes shielded by the glacis (or parapet). The rest of the elongated bastioned perimeter was massive although it had no outworks.

The buildings of the fort were to hold two infantry battalions (1600 men) and a unit of gunners together with the office-bearers from the governor down and to accommodate very large quantities of arms, equipment and supplies. the fort was admired at the time, though the design was not revolutionary, being a developed form of Vauban's popular "First System" dating from the middle of Louis XIV's reign. Its supreme importance today derives from the survival of all the defences and the complete set of internal buildings as they were raised between 1748 and 1769 to designs by Skinner and his team, and constructed by John Adam as Master Mason to the Board of Ordnance, aided in the earlier years by his brothers Robert and James. In the years while the fort was being created, there was also considerable activity on garrison buildings in Edinburgh Castle, including the barracks now transmuted into the Scottish National War Memorial.

By the time that Fort George had been completed the Jacobite threat was a thing of the past. The stronghold, however, kept a reduced garrison as did most of the other military establishments set up in the Highlands over the previous half century, while the road system constructed to support them was accepted into the pattern of civilian communication. On to this scene, created to oppose a vanished threat, came the impact of the American War of Independence, with the revolutionary colonists allied to France. In the course of the conflict Highland regiments were raised, and most of them at some stage spent a period at Fort George. There the ample and recently built accommodation proved invaluable, both then and in later wars. With hindsight this use may be seen as saving the fort from the abandonment and ruin which the disappearance of the Jacobite threat would otherwise have brought upon it.

Fort Charlotte

During the American War another threat emerged with the raids on northern England and Scotland by John Paul Jones in 1778, and coast defence, long the chief raison d'etre of fortification in the south, emerged conspicuously in Scotland with numerous batteries to protect ports and anchorages. On the eastern seaboard these extended northwards from a compact self-defensible work at Dunbar to a rebuild of the bastioned Charles II work in Shetland, renamed Fort Charlotte. The wars against revolutionary and Napoleonic France continued and developed the same pattern. There was more intensive use of Fort George, and further coastal works included an unusually large Martello tower with a triple 24-pounder emplacement at Leith, and two late Martellos which represent the final refinement of the type at Longhope in Orkney. The latter were built to protect an important assembly point for convoys from attack by United States privateers.

In addition, major barracks were provided at ancient strongholds, in Edinburgh Castle the huge New Barracks of 1796-99 (illustrated above) and in Stirling Castle a barrack block contrived from James IV's Great Hall.

In a different dimension, a few years later the viable part of the network of roads and bridges was passed to the civil authorities, so ending a chapter of military self-interest mixed with a degree of intended social benevolence. As a result, when peace came in 1815 the communications escaped the threat that soon loomed over the defensive works. Although an order of 1817 to dismantle the highland forts was countermanded, time was running out for all of the works except for the charmed life of Fort George.

Most of the nineteenth century is something of an anticlimax after the drama of the story so far, but although events were in outline a rather pale reflection of what was happening in England, in detail there are interesting variants. The 1859 coastal fort at Broughty Castle defending the Tay incorporated a restored tower-house and pretty baronial detail by the junior Royal Engineer Robert Rowand Anderson amongst its 68-pounders and shell guns. Broughty is one of the few modest Scottish contemporaries of the great programmes of fortification in the south; though in 1878-80 three miniature forts, one with caponiers, were built for the protection of the Forth on the island of Inchkeith emplacing 10-inch rifled muzzle-loading Armstrong guns. The two survivors represent the last self-defensible works in Britain. Inchkeith went on into the twentieth century to be crammed with new guns and support buildings, expressing in a concentrated form what was happening elsewhere on the Forth and the Scottish seaboard. The new guns were steel breech-loaders, no longer using gunpowder as a propellant, of a type which in essentials is still in use, and their appearance marks a suitable point at which to conclude.

On the whole, fate in recent times has been kind to the survivors of this extraordinary range of monuments and a surprising number of constructions and buildings remain in a more or less intact form to illustrate the story throughout. The list of places where something might effectively be done is not an inordinately long one and there are qualifications on some of the places that might be put on such a list. For example, in the past there has been talk of active preservation at Inchkeith, and while one sees there overall a gradual deterioration, vandalism, though it exists, is quite effectively discouraged.

The very important Dunbar blockhouse, and the extraordinary rampart crossing an inlet of the sea to join it to the main castle, is deteriorating and sooner or later the rampart will collapse. But the high estimated costs of preservation has defied good intentions in the past and I suspect would do so again in the future. In the supporting network, several by-passed bridges are being neglected, of which the most important is Garron Bridge, designed in 1747 by the third Duke of Argyll's architect, Roger Morris, to take the Cumbarton to Inveraray road across a river north of Inveraray.

On the substantial positive side, river crossings like William Adam's notable Tay Bridge are still part of the road system and so fare better. Several structures (for example Braemar Castle, one of the tower-houses that was transformed into a barracks in 1748) are looked after by private owners or local authorities. Some field monuments like the 1548 fort at Dunglass are protected by their owners' benign neglect, which is sometimes the most sympathetic way to preserve the past. A degree of neglect has perhaps served lengths of military highway disused as public thoroughfares better than the intensive use of parts of the Stirling to Fort William road, where walkers on the West Highland Way have quite badly eroded the spectacular Devil's staircase climbing out of Glencoe.

Many structures are looked after by Historic Scotland, and aside from traditional ruined "guardianship monuments" such as Threave Castle, a wide range of others has been brought into the care of its ancestor bodies from Office of Works times onward. From early in the twentieth century there were transferred from the War Office the Lowland strongholds of Dumbarton, Edinburgh and Stirling, with Blackness and Broughty Castles and Fort Charlotte in Shetland, then in 1964 Fort George itself, where the subsequent complete rehabilitation for the Ministry of Defence has very capably assured its future. There have come from private owners in the Highlands a military road bridge, one each of the 1717 and 1748 barracks, and one of the Orkney Martellos. Other bodies have made or are making significant moves. The Association for the Protection of Rural Scotland has initiated repair work on selected lesser military road bridges, and a trust has been set up to restore the barracks at Bernera, one of the group proposed in 1717, to contrast with the ruin of its sister at Ruthven in Badenoch, meticulously preserved by Historic Scotland and illustrated below.

Above: Garron Bridge, Inverary Below: Old Military Road, Inveroran

NAVAL, MILITARY AND AIRFORCE STRUCTURES IN NORTHERN IRELAND

by Ian Gailey

In Northern Ireland the legislation for the protection of ancient monuments is basically the same as that in force in the rest of the United Kingdom, although it was not until 1974 that a Historic Buildings Council was founded. Their cut-off date for recording buildings is 1914, so a great deal of interesting military structures are not documented and must be regarded as under threat.

The earliest castles in Ulster were of the motte (mound) and bailey type, an earthen mound, having a palisade and sometimes a timber tower on top. The Anglo-Norman invasion in 1169 may be regarded as the period of introduction of the military castles of stone, a small number of which were built by the Norman conquerors during the 12th and 13th centuries, in Counties Antrim and Down.

During the 14th century Anglo-Norman power in Ireland weakened, large stone castles were no longer built, superseded by the native tower house. The tower house was a derivative of the Scottish "high house" and "Peel Tower" of the Borders. In 1429 a £10 subsidy was granted to any landholder who would build a tower of 20 feet by 16 feet and at least 40 feet high. Some were surrounded by a small courtyard or bawn. These buildings are most numerous, especially in Co, Down, where they continued to be built until the 17th century.

The Planters, who followed the "Flight of the Earls", were each required to build a fortified dwelling house, the size being dictated by the number of acres they undertook to "plant". These buildings showed a strong Scottish influence, and laid out on the same general lines, they represented the final stage of the defended house. Many of course were surrounded by the archetypal bawn.

There were numerous wars in Ireland during the 17th century, but there are few examples of permanent field or coastal fortifications. Although Belfast, Carrickfergus, Coleraine, Londonderry, Newry and Monaghan were walled towns, only the walls at Londonderry (1613-18) and fragments of those at Carrickfergus survive.

The ravages of American privateers in the early decades of the 19th century led to the construction of a chain of Martello towers around the shores of Lough Swilly and Lough Foyle: these are all in a good state of preservation and a number are in use, having been converted into holiday homes.

There was no construction of fortifications during the remainder of the century and it was not until 1907 that the port of Belfast was considered of sufficient importance to have coastal defence batteries built for its protection, at Grey Point, Co. Down and Kilroot, Co. Antrim. Apart from occasional improvements at these batteries and at Dunree, Co. Donegal and the construction of aeroplane sheds at Aldergrove Airfield (1918), nothing significant was built during the First World War and up to 1939.

Barracks survive at Omagh, Armagh (1773), Londonderry, Holywood, Ballykinler (1940) and Ballymena (1930), the most interesting being the former. This group is probably under the greatest threat because, due to the security situation, they are subject to constant modification and in some cases replacement.

During the Second World War overhead protection was added to all coastal defence batteries (1940), and emergency batteries were built at Orlock, Larne and Magilligan. The threat of invasion led to the construction of "pill boxes" at strategic points all over the Province. These were built either as part of defensive lines, or for airfield defence, and many of them survive in reasonable condition.

A legacy of the Second World War is the profusion of surviving airfield architecture, some of which is quite rare. Because of its location, Northern Ireland played a most important part in the air and anti-submarine war. Latterly there were 29 operational airfields with a variety of different roles, a number of these at interesting sites such as the control tower and hospital at Langford Lodge, the flying boat dock at Castle Archdale and the dome trainer and operations block at Limavady. These are in no immediate danger, but a change in land use by the landowner could alter the situation drastically.

Dome Trainer, Limavady Airfield

There are two known anti-aircraft gun sites surviving, one at Ballymacormick and the other near Comber. These are covered with vegetation and disappear from view in the summer again and lie undisturbed at the whim of the landowner.

Northern Ireland is unique in the United Kingdom as buildings are constantly being fortified, and pill boxes being built. Great pains have been taken to make some blend in with their surroundings, one such pill box in a Belfast urban area is affectionately known as the "Wendy House".

Steps must be taken to bring the dates and type of buildings to be listed into line with the rest of the country before a great number of interesting military structures are lost.

AERODROMES AND AIR FORCE BUILDINGS

By Roger Bowdler

Britain ceased to be an island in 1906, when the first powered flight - some 722 feet long - took place in Europe. The Royal Flying Corps was founded six years later and in 1918 became the Royal Air Force. Air power has grown in importance throughout the century and has played a vital role in safeguarding the security of the nation: so much so, that the Battle of Britain actually took place in the sky several miles above south-east England in the summer of 1940. But what is the present state of Britain's military aviation heritage on the ground today?

The number of one-time aerodromes and landing grounds runs into the high hundreds, mostly dating from the Second World War. Over 360,000 acres were taken up by them in 1945. At their peak in 1942, new aerodromes were being completed at a rate of one every three days for use by the RAF and the United States Army Air Force. So vast was the quantity of concrete being poured onto the flatter parts of the British Isles during aerodrome construction that it was compared to a thirty foot wide road running from London to Peking. Tens of thousands of structures were put up, ranging from hangars to nissen huts, control towers to squash courts.

Yet the total number of military aviation structures presently listed is (by my calculation) twenty five, mostly hangars. The latest RAF building among these dates from 1920 and is the former chapel at Tangmere outside Chichester. Not a single building of Second World War vintage is listed.

The former Royal Aircraft Establishment at Farnborough contains the oldest listed buildings in the country connected with military aviation. The metal-framed Q3 building began life in 1893 as a balloon shed and was subsequently converted into offices. The list entry states that 'it is included for historical reasons as one of the oldest buildings in the world continuously associated with aviation and possibly the first to be association with flying'. This resounding description was not enough to save it from demolition in 1989. So much for the preserving power of historical interest.

What, briefly, do aerodromes consist of? A landing strip, operational and administrative buildings, and quarters. The oldest extant Royal Flying Corps buildings are at the former Central Flying School, Upavon, Wiltshire and date from 1912 onwards. Frontline First World War airfields were so impermanent that the description 'Flying Circus' alluded to their travelling canvas structures. Listed buildings of this vintage include three hangars at Duxford, outside Cambridge, of 1917-18 which were built by German prisoners of war; two pairs of hangars at Hucknall, Nottinghamshire of 1916; and two groups of hangars at the former Hendon aerodrome in North London. Save one of the latter, all of these are of a common type made of brick and concrete, with elaborate latticed 'Belfast' truss roofs of wood. The design of aerodromes was initially the responsibility of the Royal Engineers, who, ever since the eighteenth century, have been responsible for the innovative design of so many military and naval buildings.

The largest hangars of all (and probably the largest listed buildings in the country) are the pair at Cardington, Bedfordshire, which date from 1916-17 and 1928. They were built to house airships, and their vast corrugated steel masses make a hugely dramatic contribution to their arable settings.

A new period of aerodrome construction began around 1930. A separate Air Ministry had been formed in 1918 and it assumed responsibility for the design of aerodrome buildings from the R.E. Its staff were on secondment from H.M. Office of Works and thus the neo-Georgian style so familiar from inter-war telephone exchanges and post offices became the RAF style too. The grandest of all RAF buildings is the Staff College at Cranwell, Lincolnshire of 1933, by J G West FRIBA of the Office of Works. Busiest of all architects working on aerodromes was Archibald Bulloch FRIBA (active 1906-41), also of the Office of Works. Predictably, officers' messes tend to be the most architecturally ambitious buildings: of these, none surpasses that of Biggin Hill, south of Bromley, of 1930, which at the time of writing has just been put up for sale.

Above: The great aircraft hangars at Cardington, Beds

Below: The Control Tower at RAF Hullavington, Wiltshire

In 1935 the so-called Expansionist period began. Germany's bellicose resurgence under Hitler made rearmament not only politically palatable but pressingly urgent. The Versailles Treaty had banned Germany from having an air force, but in March 1935 the formation of the Luftwaffe was officially announced. Its rapid growth, and its bombing of Guernica in 1937 during the Spanish Civil War, fuelled widespread concern at the menace posed to Britain by aerial bombardment. As a result, expenditure on the RAF soared. In 1934 it just surpassed £900,000, but in 1938 it was over £20 million. The Builder for 8 April 1938 announced that the Air Ministry was about to embark upon an £11 million programme of new building, an unprecedented amount for a government department. In the nick of time, the foundations were being laid for the air defence of Britain and the waging of total war.

The scale of this challenge was vast, as was the pressure of time. Standardisation of design and the prefabrication of components were the principal means by which the challenge was met. The vast majority of Second World War RAF buildings were strictly utilitarian and temporary in nature. They thus belong more to the realms of industrial archaeology than architecture; nothing in Britain approaches the Italian airfield structures design by the high priest of concrete, Pier Luigi Nervi in 1935-42. Expenditure on buildings competed with expenditure on aeroplanes and pilots, and it was the latter two which were to be so needed in 1940.

Major developments in aircraft design in the mid-30s affected aerodrome design. Biplanes, capable of taking off from grass strips in almost all weathers, gave way to much faster, more heavily armed monoplanes. The Hawker Hurricane entered production in 1937, the Supermarine Spitfire shortly after; the biggest bomber to date, the four-engined Short Stirling, first flew in 1939.

These Dreadnoughts of the air needed longer runways, ideally of concrete, for all-weather flying. A frantic campaign of runway construction began in 1939. Generally, three runways were positioned at 60 degree angles to each other to allow for changing wind direction. Running around these was a perimeter track, around which were erected disposal pens, revetment like structures of brick and earth (with air raid shelters within) in which aircraft were parked ready for take-off and protected from all but a direct bomb blast.

Hangars of a variety of types were used for maintenance and repairs, but not for garaging the aeroplanes: keeping them together was felt to offer too tempting a target for aerial attack.

Otherwise, aerodromes of the Expansion period consisted of a blend of operational and accommodation buildings. From the late 1930s on, their neo-Georgian appearance was diminished as flat concrete bomb proof roofs replaced their pitched slate predecessors. A ring of defensive fighter stations was developed around London and the south-east: Tangmere, Hawkinge, Manston, Biggin Hill, Kenley, Northolt, Hornchurch, North Weald, Duxford and others. Their names were to become extremely well known.

The few aircraft that survive from the war are now mainly in museums. Aviation history has concentrated virtually exclusively on the aeroplanes and a newly formed body, the Airfield Research Group, has been set up to study the other survivors, aerodromes. In what sort of condition are they in today?

The great majority were decommissioned soon after the war and returned to agricultural use. Hangars and nissen huts are often used as farm buildings. In recent years the RAF has tended to concentrate at fewer, larger bases. The Options for Change Defence White Paper is bound to continue this trend. Those few airfields still used for military flying, such as the Bomber Command aerodrome at Scampton, Lincolnshire, are likely to have undergone considerable alteration (security generally precludes establishing precisely how much). Quite a few have become civil airfields: Biggin Hill now rejoices in the evocative title of Bromley Airport and its 1930s buildings survive to a remarkable degree owing to the fact that the RAF did not finally vacate the airfield until the summer of 1992. Belfast and Manchester airports began as wartime aerodromes, but little (if anything) remains at either.

Aerodromes and prisons are diametrically opposed building types, but several former RAF stations have become such : the infamous Long Kesh prison in Northern Ireland was built in 1941 as an

Inside a hangar at the Museum, RAF Duxford, Cambs

aerodrome, becoming a prison in 1971. Ford Open Prison in Sussex began life as a naval air station.

More accessible are museums. RAF Duxford is now a branch of the Imperial War Museum: the sector control room, from where aircraft were directed to their targets, is now used as a lecture hall. The RAF Museum at Hendon is impressive internally, with dozens of aircraft packed below Belfast truss roofs, but the outside is smothered in bland additions of the early 1970s, while just across the perimeter fence a group of brick buildings dating from the First World War stand idle and sand-bagged machine gun posts disintegrate. So little store is set by aviation buildings, that the world's finest collection of aircraft is cherished while a few yards away, their built counterparts fester.

At North Weald in Essex a more dynamic approach is taken: the 'Aces High' collection is housed in re-used wartime hangars, one of this has been re-erected from elsewhere.

Hawkinge, home of the Kent Battle of Britain Museum and the last untouched airfield of the Battle of Britain, has recently had approval from Shepway District Council for the construction of a housing estate and sewage works.

Many aerodromes have vanished and quite rightly too. All that is left of RAF Beaulieu Heath, for instance, is a hut now used as the East Boldre village hall. They were large and diffuse sites and thus hard to retain. In recent years, a growing number of memorials have been placed at airfield sites, but with few exceptions they are of no more than middling visual quality. Their erection, however, is a clear sign of the increasing notice being taken of these historically important sites. How much more eloquent to retain an actual part of an aerodrome - a dispersal pen (as has been done in the Hornchurch Country park, Havering) or a control tower?

One important recent development has been the creation of the country's first airfield conservation area. RAF Hullavington in Wiltshire was built in the 1930s as a major training base. Uniquely, it was faced in stone and thus presents an architecturally more attractive appearance than other RAF stations, and late last year it was accorded conservation area status. English Heritage has engaged the leading specialist in the field to produce a nationwide survey identifying exceptional airfield structures which ought to be considered for listing in the near future.

Aerodromes are a recent development and they lack the architectural quality of barracks and dockyards. Their historical importance, however, has been enormous. Britain has been lucky to have escaped conflict upon her soil for hundreds of years: aerodromes are among the few defensive buildings in the country ever to have been used in anger. It was from these places that invasion was averted: some recognition of the importance of a number of aerodromes should be made before they are all changed, and their evocative power lost for good.

THE REUSE OF MILITARY RESOURCES IN THE UNITED STATES

by William Bolger

The American experience in the reuse of defence structures dates to at least 1823. The circular masonry artillery battery in lower Manhattan, known as Castle Clinton, was sold to the City of New York and reused first as a pleasure ground. It was later roofed over and served as the city's first major concert hall, then for 35 years as it first immigration station. In 1896 it was converted into an aquarium, its fifth use in only 85 years!

In subsequent years the business of adaptive reuse has become only more complicated and rarely as picturesque. There are approximately 3,800 installations including everything from isolated missile silos to army bases containing hundreds, or even thousands of buildings. Collectively, these resources include more than twenty-four million acres and provide employment for 3.2 million people. Currently the post Cold War reduction plans call for some 86 defence sites to close by 1995. Thirty additional closures were announced this March.

While this seems to be only a small number in comparison to the total, it includes some of the nation's largest, oldest and most historic installations. In addition to this there are retirement of naval vessels and the deactivating of nuclear missile facilities called for by the various arms-limitation treaties. All this activity comes on the heels of the last major round of closures of sites (1962-77) which, in many instances, have yet to be successfully reused.

The current depression of the real estate market in much of the U.S. has further complicated the situation so that many projects are being thwarted by lack of investment capital. Projects that have moved forward are generally driven by economic development agendas which rarely pause for preservation interests. Lacking entirely is any comprehensive system that designates surplus property as museum sites, as adaptive re-use projects or some appropriate combination of the two. Nevertheless, the time-honoured method of "muddling through" has produced many projects worthy of examination and even emulation. The case studies included here illustrate some major trends and discoveries.

Arsenals

The United States Department of Defense (DOD) built and maintained its own arsenals, or munitions factories, into the 1970's. While some production facilities have been retained, many have been conveyed in whole or part to other agencies, local governments, or private corporations. These installations may not be the first to come to mind at the mention of military architecture. Yet, in a country that has not hosted major military conflict on its soil since 1865, arsenals offer some of the most tangible evidence of our military past. In fact, Franklin D Roosevelt labelled America "the great arsenal of democracy". A walk through one of these sites reveals a clear and powerful record of that role. The architecture of arsenals combines the aesthetic and structural character of military engineering in an industrial setting. Rarely will you find manufacturing structures erected with so little concern for cost. The resulting works are both impressive and enduring.

The arsenal in Springfield, Massachusetts, which was established in 1794, became one of the first to be closed in 1968 and converted to new uses. The site, covering 280 acres, was divided into five development parcels. Of these, three were considered to be historically important and were listed on the National Register of Historic Places. A 55 acre tract received the added distinction of being declared a National Historic Landmark - considered by the government to be of national importance and within this was created the Springfield Armory National Historic Site dedicated to preserving the armory collection. The remainder was conveyed to the Springfield Technical College with the intention of using existing buildings for college needs. These classifications set the stage for different treatments and reuses, with non Landmark land given over to industrial development. Although Springfield stands as a significant attempt to approach the preservation of such large facilities over time this reuse has proven disappointing in many respects. New buildings have been constructed while historic buildings have remained vacant or even been demolished.

The Frankford Arsenal in Philadelphia became redundant fifteen years after Springfield, at a time when there were virtually no public funds for non-profit preservation projects. All but a small part of the site was placed on the National Register and conveyed to a private development firm which has redeveloped the complex as an industrial park. This approach has had the advantage of maintaining a single owner/manager for the property while allowing for a variety of tenants. Historic preservation controls have been applied at both local and national levels. The City of Philadelphia exercises exterior design control of project work while the Federal government controls all rehabilitation work under the provisions of the transfer.

Tax incentives have helped greatly: under the National Economic Recovery Tax Act of 1981, 25% investment tax relief was allowed to developers of historic properties. This credit, which could be passed through to limited partners, was enormously successful in attracting investment capital to historic resources (although in 1986 the tax incentives were reduced considerably). In general the Frankford reuse has proven successful from both an economic and preservation perspective.

Buildings at the Frankford Arsenal, undergoing conversion

Two other arsenal reuse projects are located in Watertown, Massachusetts and Pittsburgh, Pennsylvania. The Watertown property of 40 acres was also divided among a number of different owners and has been under redevelopment since the 1970's. The former officers' club and carpentry shop buildings were adapted by the Harvard Community Health Plan Corporation as a medical centre. This new use demanded fairly dramatic changes to the buildings including a covered link, a new stair and elevator tower and disabled access. The conversion scheme designed by architects Steffian Bradley Associates of Boston is visually strong and functional with costs at a reasonable $125 per square foot. The new elements make a clear contemporary statement. They do, however, pose a critical question to "preservationists" as to when new design statements are desirable and when the reuse should be subordinate to the historic design.

In Pittsburgh, at the now vacant Hays Ammunition Plant, the Urban Redevelopment Authority is working with the Pittsburgh film office to use the plant as a motion picture sound stage. They elieve that this is a use specifically suited to take advantage of the building's chief characteristics:

Historic buildings at the Watertown Arsenal, Massachusetts, before (above) and after (below) conversion to a medical centre

a large open space of some 180,000 square feet with a 60 foot high interior. In this instance the local government is actively pursuing a reuse suited for the resource rather than passively offering it for development. Results of a marketing study assessing economic factors are due later this year.

In general, an important factor which most developers have cited regarding the reuse of military facilities is the advantage they offer in terms of planning approvals. As existing facilities they often already have permission for even the most intense industrial uses. While many communities resist the creation of new areas for development, the reuse of existing sites can create jobs and boost the local economy.

Armories

The most ubiquitous of defense structures, armories, are found throughout the US on army bases as well as in towns and cities where they served the training needs of National Guard units and the army reserves. They present a strong and even picturesque military facade combined with a functional large open interior space. These sites are often used for intermittent civilian activities even when still on active duty. (The 69th Regiment Armory in New York City houses the famous International Exhibition of Modern Art in 1913.)

Their frequent reuse is not surprising and frequently goes unnoticed. Occasionally the reuses are very dramatic as in the case of Richmond Virginia's Blues Armory. A downtown redevelopment project in the mid-1980's incorporated the armory into a shopping mall by building a three storey glass addition connecting the north facade of the armory to adjacent buildings. The treatment, which the developers insisted was essential for project marketability, nevertheless resulted in the loss of the investment tax credit. Federal preservation officials reviewing the project held that a primary facade had been compromised by making it an interior wall, and that the free-standing independent character of the structure had been violated. This seemed an especially egregious treatment for a fortress, or even a pseudo-fortress.

The Hyattsville Armory in Maryland exemplifies its type in style and function as well as in its history of use. Based on a Medieval English castle design and situated on a hill overlooking the town, the armory is known locally as "The Castle". Following the departure of the first Maryland Infantry's Company F, the building was used as office and storage space, a roller rink, and a meeting place for local organisations. In the mid-1980s it was adapted for use as the Castle Center for the Performing Arts which included a 300-seat theatre, plus large restaurant and office space. Oehrlein and Associates of Washington DC developed a redesign approach with an addition that is subordinate to the 1918 structure. The interior, while greatly altered, is compatible with the character of the military design. This project maintains uses which are community oriented, thus preserving not only the structure but its role as a civic focus of the Hyattsville community.

Army Forces and Air Bases

The scale of these resources makes it difficult to assess preservation treatments and results. Comparable to towns and even small cities these facilities are rarely subject to any single reuse. The major factors effecting reuses range from location (urban versus rural), community economic development needs and environmental clearance requirements. Urban facilities are often subject to high pressure development demands while rural ones often have low market demands resulting in disuse.

Of the hundred or so bases that were closed during the period 1961 to 1986 the three principal new uses found were educational institutions, industrial and office parks and air parks (small airports). In some instances, while preservation was not an intentional goal, it was achieved to a surprising degree. At Fort Dupont in Delaware, one of the port defences for Philadelphia, a state psychiatric hospital for young people made use of most of the buildings for the same functions as originally intended. The chapel, auditorium, gymnasium, barracks, houses and the hospital needed little, if any, changes.

Without a preservation commitment, however, many important historic structures have been lost or are threatened. Fort Hancock, at the entrance to New York City's outer harbour, was given directly to the National Park Service, but only for the purpose of recreation and nature conservation (i.e. the beaches and dunes). There has been no budget or directive for the redevelopment of the roughly one hundred fort buildings even though they have been recognised as a National Historic Landmark.

In order for large sites to be preserved in ways that retain essential historic character as well as specific key resources, intensive planning is needed well in advance of closing. At the Presidio (meaning fort or garrison), an army base in San Francisco which was established originally by the Spanish in 1776, the National Park Service is heading just such an effort. The base, which is scheduled to close by 1995, occupies some of the most valuable and spectacular real estate anywhere in the country. The need for an overall plan that would respect both natural and historic resources was recognised over twenty years ago and when the closure of the base was finally announced in 1989 the N.P.S. planning effort was already under way. An intricate year-by-year process was established to include a wide range of consultation with, and involvement by, all possible concerned parties. As of late 1992 the N.P.S. had begun to receive its first preliminary proposals for redevelopment.

Above: View from the Golden Gate Bridge in San Francisco looking south at the Presidio

The Presidio's standing as an historic preservation project as well as an economic development owes everything to the enduring interest that it has held for San Franciscans. Not all resources that are deserving of preservation have enjoyed such widespread public awareness and interest. Indeed, many military facilities have intentionally existed behind impenetrable security shields. The U.S. Congress in recognising the need to promote the assessment and awareness of military resources, established the Cold War Task Force and the Legacy Program. Legacy has programme managers inside the Department of Defense who are funded to undertake assessments of all resources, both archival and architectural or structural and to promote preservation.

One pilot project funded by Legacy holds particular promise. The Rocky Mountains - Great Plains Regional Office of the National Trust for Historic Preservation is currently studying military installations within its ten- state region to identify and analyse partnerships between the military and local organisations which promote resource identification, interpretation and preservation. The premise of the study is that without local grass roots involvement in military historic sites there will be no room for preservation at the negotiating table when the resources become available. In studying successful partnerships that have occurred "spontaneously" the Trust hopes to identify strategies for repeating successful experiences elsewhere.

Naval Shipyards and Naval Vessels

Naval shipyards combine the qualities of military bases and industrial manufacturing in maritime settings to produce one of the most appealing and desirable types of defence resources. The leading example for the adaptive reuse of shipyards is in Boston. The Charlestown Navy Yard, which closed in the mid 1970s, was the subject of an intense planning effort similar to the Presidio. The project is nearly complete and comprises a full preservation zone - part of Boston National Historic Park, a zone where, together with the conversion of existing buildings, new buildings will be permitted, developed by private corporations, and a new construction zone.

Some of the historic structures intended for reuse have been slow finding new tenants, such as the rope walk and the chain forge, which pose practical difficulties for most modern needs. Other features within the historic site have proven too costly and impractical to save. Overall the results have been very successful. In retrospect, the only major aspect of the yard's original character not be retained is the presence of actual naval vessels. While portions of the waterfront were developed as a marina for recreational craft, these diminutive civilian vessels are hardly capable of evoking the spirit of their distant relatives.

It seems especially unfortunate that no naval vessels were retained at the yard considering their wide public appeal. Last year a number of U.S. cities competed for possession of the aircraft carrier USS Lexington, one of the best known combatants of the Second World War. It was finally awarded to Corpus Christy, Texas, where they expect it to attract over 300,000 visitors a year. In New York City, the USS Intrepid has become one of the most popular historic attractions in the city with an annual visitation of 500,000 people. Combining shipyard preservation with either interpreted ships or mothballed fleets in future projects should be a key goal.

The Military Resource as Museum

Those in the conservation world have long understood that in order to responsibly advocate the protection of all deserving historic and cultural resources their economic value must be realised. In other words, we cannot afford to support all worthy historic sites as museums. Nevertheless, some sites and objects, or aspects of the same, can only survive as such. When viewed in the broader context of a community, museum operations often offer secondary economic returns from increased tourism or the less tangible benefits of image and identity.

Most of the great masonry fortifications of the eighteenth and nineteenth century have long since passed from the DOD to federal, state, local and non-profit sectors for use as historic sites. Even Castle Clinton has been restored by the National Park Service as an historic site. The scenic and historic values that these structures possess, along with the impracticality of any economic reuse, recommends them for historic site designation. They are also truly "landmarks" within their regions. As we have already noted, resources such as aircraft carriers and battleships can often demonstrate economic returns for their communities. It is significant, with respect to the National Trust partnership survey, that one of the most outstanding museum projects in recent years has been the result of one man's foresight and perseverance in association with a local air museum.

In the early 1980's, when the Titan missile system was deactivated in accordance with SALT agreements, all 54 silos and their associated control structures were to be totally destroyed. No one at the national, state or local levels proposed preserving a single silo for posterity. One individual, Lieutenant Colonel (retired) Orville Dougherty, a former wing commander at the

Arizona Titan group, resolved that one silo would survive. The task required the approval of the National Security Council as well as the USSR's arms negotiators. The resulting Titan Missile Museum in Green Valley Arizona is the only Intercontinental Ballistic Missile museum in the world. It stands today complete in every detail "as a memorial to the thousands of Air Force members who dedicated untold hours in lonely missile sites throughout the United States".

The thirty thousand visitors who tour the Arizona site annually, approach the site's practical capacity. However, other more recently deactivated systems may benefit from the example. The National Park Service is now studying the Titan museum to determine the feasibility of museum use of one Minute Man Missile site in South Dakota. If the destructive threat of these weapons is finally behind us, and we in fact do have a future, then these sites will surely be among the greatest documents of our age.

FUTURE
UNCERTAIN?

ROYAL ARSENAL, WOOLWICH

The Woolwich Dockyard, founded in the mid fifteenth century, flourished under Henry VIII but by 1869 Devonport had taken over in importance and the Dockyard closed. Meanwhile, an adjacent riverside site then known as Woolwich Warren, was purchased by the Crown in 1671, for use initially as an ordnance storage depot, developing into a munitions factory by the end of the century.

In 1696 the Royal Laboratory was founded, with two ranges of buildings - pavilions and workshops around a courtyard. Two buildings survive today and they are the earliest on the site.

In 1716 the Royal Brass Foundry was established at Woolwich as the first of several major building projects: Dial Square, a complex of buildings and workshops servicing the foundry; the carriage storehouse and houses for the Arsenal's senior officers and barracks and accommodation for the newly formed Royal Artillery regiment.

The Arsenal grew at a rapid pace throughout the eighteenth century and the area covered increased to 104 acres. The wall, built in 1804, by convict labour, ran for two and a half miles. By this time the Royal Ordnance Factory had been established.

The architect James Wyatt was appointed architect to the Board of Ordnance by the Duke of Richmond in 1782 and his work at Woolwich has been described by the historian John Martin Robinson as "splendid examples of austere neo-classical architecture" with his Grand Store as "the most magnificent warehouse complex in England". Together with the work of Vanbrugh the architecture of Woolwich Arsenal is of more than national importance.

In the nineteenth century the Crimean War saw increased activity in the production of guns and ammunition at Woolwich and in 1860 new steam driven machinery was introduced. Experimentation and invention in weaponry advanced rapidly, needing more and more industrial buildings, a gasholder, iron pier, crane and pits.

Similarly, production increased to meet needs created by the Boer War and the Great War. By 1907 the Royal Arsenal had grown to over 1200 acres, at its peak employing 80,000 people.

By the time the Second World War broke out munitions factories had developed elsewhere in the country although Woolwich was still a key producer of armaments: guns, tanks and explosives.

In peacetime activities at Woolwich reduced and operations wound down rapidly in comparison with the 300 year growth of the establishment. The Royal Ordnance Factory closed in 1967. Since then it has been in partial use by the MoD and they will vacate the site at the end of 1995.

Although the Arsenal was surveyed for listed building purposes in 1973 many important mid-Victorian buildings were omitted and have since been torn down, these include some early cast iron framed warehouses. Security at the site has long prevented inspections of the historic buildings by experts and historians and that must be why so much that was of enormous interest has been undervalued, lost or neglected for so long.

What will happen to the Arsenal - and in particular to its eighteen listed buildings (several of outstanding importance) - is very much under consideration at present, and the site is due to be marketed by agents Hillier Parker. Together with the London Borough of Greenwich, a planning brief has been drawn up outlining possible uses for the various parts of the site including some use by the University of Greenwich, retail, housing, museum and tourism.

There has been great concern about the condition of some of the listed buildings for many years. Most stand in the western part of the site. Having been in Crown ownership (exempt from normal listed building controls and responsibilities) much has been demolished; several of the surviving buildings have been totally abandoned to decay, whilst others have (frustratingly) been restored in a somewhat over zealous manner. This is all the more reason that a close watch be kept on proposals for the buildings that survive.

The two pavilions that stand in isolated positions facing each other are the earliest buildings in the Arsenal, dating from 1696, and are all that remain of the Royal Laboratory. Excellent documentary evidence survives showing the range of buildings that once stood round the quadrangle. The identical buildings, (though one has lost its central pediment) are listed grade II, but are in a pitiful condition and should be a priority for repair and restoration as centrepieces when the site changes hands.

VERBRUGGEN'S HOUSE

The Verbruggen brothers were Master Founders of the Arsenal and this very handsome house was specially built as their residence in 1772 (following their complaints about the former Founder's house). It has had a range of uses and has been much altered inside, however it is now in good condition and is listed grade II.

DIAL ARCH BLOCK

This is all that is left of 'The Great Pile', a complex built in 1717 round two squares, encompassing washing, turning and engraving processes. The architect is probably Vanbrugh. What survives is a single storey block with extremely fine brickwork with an impressive central pedimented gateway over which a sundial was placed in 1764. The Dial Arch, which is listed grade II, was restored by the PSA in the 1980's.

ACADEMY BUILDING

Also known as the Officers' Quarters, or The Model Room, it replaced an earlier Tudor building in 1716-20 and was probably designed by Vanbrugh. The first Royal Military Academy was housed here until it moved to Woolwich Common in 1806. The building became a museum and later the Pattern Room of the Royal Laboratory. After the Second World War it became the officers' mess for personnel working on the site. It is a striking building, listed grade II*. Either side of the central frontispiece stand two circular pedestals supporting a lion and a unicorn. It is believed these may have been part of the entrance to the Royal Laboratory.

One of the most important buildings, of 1717 by Vanbrugh and listed grade I, the Foundry was restored by the PSA in 1968-70, but in a heavy handed manner. The work has been criticised for its crude brickwork, inappropriate window designs and internal alterations. Nevertheless, it remains a very important and attractive building in very fine multicoloured stock brickwork with Portland stone dressings. Above the impressive entrance is the Royal coat of arms and the building is crowned by a lantern clad in lead. The Foundry is used as archives for the National Maritime Museum.

THE GRAND STORE

The Grand Store was designed by James and Lewis Wyatt in 1805 and built between 1806-13. It was built at enormous expense on driven piles to service the new river wharf and was one of the most ambitious buildings in the history of the Arsenal. It consists of three huge ranges of brick and ashlar storehouses round a central court, the fourth side open to the river. Infill buildings of a later date now occupy the central space, but they have not diminished the grandeur of the Wyatts' design.

Despite suffering from structural problems and subsidence in 1832, attempts to dismantle the storehouse were resisted on the grounds, "that they form an imposing structure, are conveniently sited and are a credit to the naval and military reputation of the country".

Most of the store has been abandoned over the years and part now has a temporary roof. The Grand Store is acknowledged as unquestionably the single most important surviving structure of the nineteenth century at Woolwich and to have been deliberately neglected for so long is scandalous. It also deserves an upgrading from its grade II status.

THE RINK

This was the most important industrial building in the Arsenal, developed from 1876, the great radial crane was roofed over in 1891. It had a lifting capacity of 50 tons and was not replaced until 1939.

GUN SHRINKING PITS

The mid nineteenth century pits were in the open ground and later covered by massive, elaborate iron structures. This has all disappeared together with other machinery such as the huge steam hammer and furnace.

OFFICERS' QUARTERS

A handsome three storey Georgian terrace, dating from the early eighteenth century, it may well have been part of the original Vanbrugh period scheme for Dial Square. It's demolition in the early 1980's damaged the layout of the square, opening up and isolating buildings such as the Verbruggen House.

CADET QUARTERS

These two ranges of housing were built in 1751 for cadets of the Royal Military Academy and were enlarged to the designs of Wyatt in the 1780's - his first work at the Arsenal. They stood on the south west boundary of the site, by the main gate. A most attractive terrace, with front gardens enclosed by iron railings, they were pulled down to make way for the widening of the Plumstead Road.

There are several other historic buildings at Woolwich for which new uses need to be found as part of the overall redevelopment. These include:

Armstrong Gun Factory - only the facade has been retained (with a modern building behind). The factory was built in 1856 to meet the demands of the Crimean War, housing a large foundry and boring mill for the manufacture of the armstrong gun - a revolutionary breech loading weapon and a great technological breakthrough. What remains is listed grade II.

Middlegate House - a substantial early nineteenth century house listed grade II, situated by the Middlegate of the Arsenal on the north east edge.

Officers Quarters - there was at one time much more surviving of the early eighteenth century accommodation for officers. This remaining building stands just off what was Dial Square.

The Riverside Guardrooms - twin octagonal buildings of 1814-15 situated on the river as part of the defences of the Arsenal. Only one retains its conical low pitched roof. Listed grade II.

New Laboratory Square (east wing) - only one range survives of the original four that made up the Square. They were built in 1806-10 as additional laboratory accommodation and are thought to be more work of the Wyatts. Unfortunately the three blocks were demolished before they could be listed.

New Carriage Store - present buildings replaced earlier stores in 1778, whilst Wyatt replaced the long north front in 1802. This has a pedimented central portion surmounted by a clock turret. The Store has been altered and extended substantially but is listed grade II.

New Carriage Store

Only one range survives of the four that made up New Laboratory Square. Below is one of the demolished blocks.

This great impressive building, begun in 1775, is a shrine to the history of the gunners. Pevsner compares the scale of the grand parade only to St Petersburg, for its facade is over 1,000 feet long. The row of six three storey typical Georgian blocks in yellow stock brick are connected by colonnades. They face south over the Common towards the Academy. Behind the main building are buildings and barrack blocks of a later date.

Changes within the regiment of the Royal Artillery mean much of their buildings are no longer required and although they hope to keep a presence, most of this complex will need to find a new occupier.

The facade is temporarily covered in scaffolding for essential repairs

The Academy for the Royal Artillery regiment was originally situated within the Royal Arsenal but moved to its present site in 1805. Here, on Woolwich common, James Wyatt designed a huge and elaborate complex in a suitably castellated style. The long north front, stretching 720 feet, has a central "keep" modelled on the Tower of London, with four turrets at each corner. At either end are later pavilions and yet more buildings behind.

The Academy has long been known as "the shop" to those who trained there, but it has ceased as a military academy and is only partly used for offices. The Royal Artillery have less and less use for the buildings and its disposal is likely to be sought in the future. An educational use would be the most appropriate.

THE SMALL ARMS FACTORY, ENFIELD

The history of the Small Arms Factory at Enfield dates back to the latter years of the Napoleonic wars. The Enfield site was chosen for its close proximity to the Government owned gunpowder works at Waltham Abbey, and because its river offered both easy transportation to the arsenal at the Tower of London, and a ready supply of energy to run the machines. Though John Rennie was commissioned to draw up plans for the site, it appears that the buildings were mostly designed by John By, RE.

Nothing of the early nineteenth century factory has survived, the buildings we see today date primarily from an 1850's build. The poor performance of British guns during the Crimean War was a cause of great concern to the Government and in 1854 a select committee decision led to the complete re-building of the Enfield factory. It was built from 1854-58 at a total cost of £150,000. An American armourer and three artificiers were hired to teach the skills used in making the more advanced American rifles and led to the development of the famous Lee Enfield rifle.

The Factory continued in use until 1988. British Aerospace purchased the site from the Government and, forming a consortium with Trafalgar House, made plans for its redevelopment but so far nothing has happened. The historic buildings have now stood empty, disused and unmaintained for too long, their condition is deteriorating. A scheme that offers the buildings a new life, without compromising their historic integrity, is urgently needed.

The machine shop, interior and exterior

THE GUNPOWDER MILLS, WALTHAM ABBEY

The manufacture of gunpowder at Waltham Abbey is known to date from at least the seventeenth century and there may well have been an industry in the area in late medieval times. The site was acquired for the crown in 1787 and since that time it has grown rapidly, ever changing with the developments in the manufacture of gunpowder. During the Napoleonic Wars the factory supplied the Royal Arsenal at Woolwich with 25,000 barrels of explosives a year and in the latter years of the First World War it employed a workforce of 5,000, over half of whom were women.

The Gunpowder Mills, which have been used since the Second World War for research and development, were closed down in 1991. The MOD have commissioned a number of studies to assess the importance of the site and the possibilities for its future use including tourism. One problem is the site's contamination with chemicals, explosive materials and asbestos. A recent study for the MOD ominously suggested, "Decontamination....may require the virtual demolition and burning of the buildings....yet it is these man made artefacts that could best tell the story of gunpowder."

Besides its historic importance as a production site of black powder, the Waltham Abbey mills chart the transition from the manufacture of old explosive types to latterday forms of high explosives such as nitro-glycerine.

The RCHME have recently completed an archaeological survey of the Mills. Their forthcoming report on the site, which will reveal the full extent of the sites historic importance, should help to ensure that those making decisions over the future of the site are better informed. The MOD have yet to lodge a planning application, though although it would appear that provisional planning approval has been given to the idea of developing the site as a tourist attraction.

The Mills

Staging Post and Bridge

The row of magazines before demolition

This grade II listed late eighteenth century gunpowder magazine is one of the last surviving remnants of the Purfleet garrison. Its four neighbouring magazine's were demolished in the late 1960's and their site used for council housing. The area now has a distinctly run down appearance and no 5 magazine, standing empty and disused, is frequently subjected to vandalism. Its owners, Thurrock Borough Council are keen to install a new use to secure its future. However, new uses for this building, with two foot thick walls and an attic space lined with sand, so as to withold any explosions, could be hard to find. The council would prefer a community use. The Garrison (council) Estate, currently making a bid to the Government for funds to improve the area, are using the boarded up magazine as a flagship to champion their cause.

The sole remaining magazine, No 5, next to the new housing

SHOEBURYNESS: THE OLD RANGES

Shoeburyness was selected as a suitable location for artillery experiments in the 1840's, replacing Plumstead Marshes as a larger and more secluded site. Experiments began in 1850 and the Establishment gradually expanded with more land being purchased and gun emplacements and buildings being constructed. In 1859 the first British School of Gunnery was formed at Shoeburyness and a major building programme commenced. Most of the buildings on the site known as the Old Ranges date from this time.

The design and development of artillery weapons progressed dramatically from the 1860's, most especially the breech loading and quick firing guns and the armoured tank. In 1915 Foulness Island was purchased for further long range artillery trials and the site known as the New Ranges developed here. The Proof and Experimental Establishment at Shoeburyness occupies this site and some of the buildings at the Old Ranges, however others here are no longer required and the Ministry of Defence is seeking to dispose of them.

HORSESHOE BARRACKS

The eight separate barrack blocks dating from 1860-69 were built to form a horseshoe around a central parade ground and facing the Gatehouse. Each of two storeys with a single storey extension either side, they form a most attractive group. They are built of stock brick with slate roofs and each building has a range of ten large sash windows. Considering they have been empty since 1986 they are in remarkably good condition. There is hardly a slate missing or window broken. Toward the centre of the parade ground is a building dating from the 1930s which could be removed to restore the barracks to their original layout.

A scheme was prepared with the MOD's agents, Cluttons, for a residential conversion which was was generally welcomed by the local authority although planning consent has not yet formally been granted. Shoeburyness is approximately one hour's train journey from London and the Horseshow Barracks would convert very well to houses and flats of varying sizes, all facing onto the large landscaped central courtyard.

Together with adjacent buildings on Hospital Road the whole site being marketed is about 13.5 acres and although it is at present within the P&EE separate access and boundaries will be arranged.

GATEHOUSE & CLOCK TOWER

The three arched Gatehouse is a formal entrance to the Horseshoe Barracks. It housed the former regimental offices and guard room and was built in 1856. It is of yellow stock brick with paler coloured brick details - such as the voussoirs, or tops of the arches, and the cornices. The clock tower above has a handsome clock face on four sides surmounted by a lantern housing the bell.

FORMER GARRISON HOSPITAL AND OFFICERS' HOUSING

The hospital stands at the centre of a delightful low Georgian terrace of officers' housing all designed by George Smith & Sons of Pimlico. It was built in 1856 and is perfectly symmetrical with two single storey wings either side. It has an attractive stone built porch with stucco cornice and pilasters and a venetian window above. There is nice ironwork - railings and decorative cast iron brackets below the eaves. The officers housing was constructed a couple of years later, in similar style, all single storey, again of brick with slate roofs. Each has a front wall with gate. They could make very desirable small cottages.

Horseshoe Barracks (above), Officer Terrace along Hospital Road (below)

Colchester's 1860's Cavalry Barracks have only been partially used in recent years. Last fully occupied some ten or so years ago, they have since only been used for exercises. The red brick buildings are in a sorry state of repair. However, they have been promised a temporary reprieve as a base for troops returning from Germany. It is understood that the buildings will be restored in the near future.

The prospects for Colchester's military hospital, built 1896-9, are less bright. A couple of years ago the operating theatre and children's ward were demolished: but for the timely intrusion of the Gulf War, it is thought that the whole hospital would have been levelled. Though three quarters of the military hospital buildings still stand, and in fact continue in use as a medical welfare centre, their future remains in question.

THE CHAPEL OF THE ESSEX AND ROYAL ANGLIAN REGIMENT, WARLEY

Besides its obvious architectural merit, Warley Chapel is an interesting military rarity. As regimental chapels are usually found within nearby churches or cathedrals, it is a matter of great pride to the Essex and Royal Anglian Regiment that besides the Guards, they are the only regiment to have their own freestanding chapel.

In the summer of 1857 the East India Company commissioned Matthew Digby Wyatt to design a large chapel seating six hundred worshippers. The Romanesque style chapel, built of yellow brick with red brick dressings, was completed by December 1857.

The chapel was regarded as a garrison church until 1925, when Major General F Ventris made his successful application to the MOD for the conversion of its status from garrison to regimental chapel. the grade II listed building which continues to be regularly used, is a living regimental museum; in its nave hang thirty of the regimental colours and the mid nineteenth century pew ends are ornately carved in the memory of individual officers.

However, in the current round of cuts, the maintenance costs of the chapel will be less easy to justify than those on other military buildings amd the Regiment are concerned for the future of their fine chapel.

THE DRILL HALL, ARNOLD STREET, LOWESTOFT

This charming drill hall was built in 1871 for the training of the 1st Suffolk Artillery Volunteers. Its simple brick facade is punctuated with carved details of a strictly military type, and though it has been used as a garage for many years, the frontage design remains a potent reminder of its original purpose.

The possible listing of the drill hall is under review at present but the likely implementation of the proposed route for the Lowestoft Eastern Relief Road threatens the rear half of the building. It is thought, however, that the front portion of the old drill hall will remain in use as a garage.

Though first built in the 1540's, rebuilt in 1724 and again from 1717-20, the vast majority of the structure of the extant Landguard Fort is of an 1875 build. The square planned four bastioned fort, designed to provide protection for Harwich Harbour, lay redundant for many years before being taken into the care of the Ministry of Works in 1975. They and their successors, English Heritage, have since carried out repairs to make the fort's roof watertight. The casemates have been boarded up and the gun ports filled to protect the interiors from further decay. However, though Landguard Fort is structurally sound and temporarily protected from the elements, it still awaits restoration. It is thought to be one of the buildings currently under consideration for disposal by English Heritage.

The Royal Commission's recommendation to erect a line of forts to protect Chatham from the landward side was delayed and modified and it was only in the mid 1870's that construction work began on the four forts, Borstall, Bridgewoods, Horsted and Luton. Fort Borstall, the western most of the group, was built from 1875-83. Originally designed with its guns in fixed positions, the fort was altered during construction to enable the guns to be moved as the tactical situation demanded.

It was used during the First World War as a barracks for troops on their way to France and it housed an important anti-aircraft battery during the Second World War. Afterwards the fort passed to the Home Office who used some of the buildings for storage and turned the rest of the site into a farm. Under-maintained, the fort deteriorated rapidly. In 1990 the fort was sold to a group of businessmen who had plans to convert the buildings to a mixed industrial, residential and museum use. Though permission for their scheme was refused on grounds of access, a recent application, to convert two of the casemates into residential units with a goat farm on the rest of the site, has been accepted. The owners continue to negotiate with English Heritage over the future of the dilapidated scheduled monument.

CLIFFE FORT, CLIFFE, KENT

Cliffe Fort was built in the 1860's as a result of the findings of the 1859 Royal Commission study into the effectiveness of the coastal defences. With Coalhouse Fort across the estuary in Essex, Cliffe Fort was designed to repel any enemy attempting to sail up the Thames. The semi-circular fort is similar in type and date to Forts Darnet and Hoo which guarded the entrance to the Medway.

Now owned by Blue Circle Industries, who have mining interests in the area, Cliffe Fort languishes in disuse. Derelict and deteriorating, its future is uncertain. Also suffering and under the same ownership is the late nineteenth century Brennan torpedo station. The Brennan Torpedo, invented in 1873 by Louis Brennan, was the forerunner of all wire-guided missiles. Blue Circle are currently discussing with English Heritage the future of the scheduled monument and the Brennan Station.

Launching Bay of the Brennan Torpedo Station

Fort Darnet

The twin forts of Darnet and Hoo are located on islands about a mile apart either side of the river Medway. The 1860's forts, designed to guard the seaward approach to Chatham, were built as a result of the 1859 Royal Commission. Work commenced on the circular forts in 1861 but, owing to design alterations and problems with flooding and subsidence, they were not completed until 1871.

Last used during the Second World War, Darnet and Hoo have since stood empty and disused. Various schemes have been mooted from time to time, but have come to nothing. The scheduled monuments continue to deteriorate: a question mark hangs over their future.

Fort Hoo

The opening lines of the English Heritage description for this ancient monument read thus:

"For sheer richness of style this Victorian dock pumping station would be hard to equal. Certainly it is the finest example of its period to survive in a Royal Dockyard."

Constructed in 1873 as part of the Victorian extension of Chatham Dockyard, the imaginatively designed two storey arcaded building housed the pump that drained water from the adjacent dry dock. Built of red and white brick ornamented with blue decorative bricks, it continued to serve its original function until the early 1980's when the dockyard was closed down. It has since stood disused and there is now widespread concern as to the condition of its brickwork. Though English Estates, the new owners of the Victorian Dockyard, have no immediate plans for the building, they hope to find a new use in the future.

The grade II listed Former Officers' Mess, otherwise known as the White House, has been empty and disused for well over a decade. The theft of lead from the valley gutters has caused considerable damp problems throughout the timber framed and weather boarded structure. Fortunately, the draught from smashed windows has ventilated the building, preventing a serious case of dry rot.

The MOD had plans to demolish the mid nineteenth century building but the site is about to be transferred to Kent County Council. Though part of the barracks site will be lost in the proposed Maidstone "spine" road, the council intend to restore the Former Officers' Mess to new use. A survey to assess the condition of the building has recently been carried out by Donald Insall & Associates. Kent County Council are keen to hear from any one who might be interested in taking on the building.

THE ROYAL MARINES DEPOT, DEAL

The Officers' Mess, South Barracks

The R M Depot at Deal is a large and complex site brimming with historic buildings, four of which are listed. Its future is uncertain. Costly maintenance programmes have been put on ice, awaiting the outcome of the ongoing Band Service Study which will determine the future of the depot. After the inevitable cuts it will be yet more difficult to justify the continued existence of the Royal Marines School of Music at their current premises.

The Deal Barracks are split into three groups, North, South and East Barracks. Though there is some confusion as to the exact date of their construction, it is generally assumed that North and South Barracks date from the late eighteenth century and that East Barracks, built as an hospital dates from c1812. Built to house the infantry and cavalry, the first inhabitants of the cavalry barracks were the famous 15th Light Dragoons. It was only in 1869 that the site became Admiralty property and the Royal Marines were installed.

Though some are in need of urgent maintenance, the historic barrack buildings at Deal have escaped demolition, so common at other depots, and are in a remarkably complete state. Supplemented by numerous Victorian buildings, they create a unique historic setting. The forty acre site boasts only one twentieth century building.

Over the last twenty years the Royal Marine presence at Deal has been drastically reduced from 3,000 personnel to 300. Realistically, it is only a matter of time before the barracks will be vacated completely. Long overdue restoration work is urgently needed on most of the buildings, most particularly to the grade II listed old hospital building which suffers from dry rot.

The Royal Marines School of Music

The Royal Marines School of Music

The military presence at Stoughton Barracks declined rapidly during the 1980's: by the end of the decade they were completely unused. The brick buildings, which have since stood empty but secure, are soon to be put on the market. Outline planning consent has recently been granted for 190 residential units to be built on the site and many of the 1876 buildings will be demolished. Provisions have been made for the retention of the officers' mess (for residential use) and the keep (for residential, office or community use) and it is hoped that the barrack blocks might be retained. Recent attempts to get the officers' mess and the keep listed proved unsuccessful but they are in a conservation area and consent is needed to demolish them.

The austere keep at Stoughton Barracks is almost identical in design to the Cardwell keeps at Oxford, Reading and Lincoln. Though the Oxford keep was demolished in the early 1960's, both Reading and Lincoln keeps have been protected by listing whilst Stoughton has not.

Peninsular Barracks, the former home of the Rifle Brigade and more recently the Light Division, boasts seven listed buildings. However, five of these have stood empty since the site was vacated by the military six years ago. There are already signs of deterioration and the magnificent red brick buildings, which occupy a prime site in the centre of Winchester, are in urgent need of a new use.

There has been a military presence here since the reign of William the Conqueror. The demise of Winchester's Castle came during the Civil War when in 1656 Cromwell's forces completely demolished the Royalist stronghold. After the Restoration Charles II decided to erect a royal palace on the site. The foundation stone to the Wren designed palace, was laid in 1683 but work ceased within two years, the king had died, enthusiasm for the project had waned and there were no funds.

Work resumed in the eighteenth century and the Hampshire Chronicle of 29th of April, 1758 reports, "The palace begun by Charles II, but not finished, is now completely refitted for barracks, in which there are no less than 160 rooms." In fact it was used for foreign prisioners until the end of the century when the barrack use was resumed and in the early nineteenth century it was further altered.

On the 19th of December 1894 a savage fire, fanned by high winds, completely gutted the historic buildings and most of the fabric was destroyed.

What we see today of the Upper Peninsular Barracks was thus constructed at the turn of this century. In classical design, of red brick with stone dressings and quoins, it echoes many features from the design of the Kings House.

Upper Barracks

Lower Barracks

Some thirty yards from the imposing new home of the Rifle Brigade were erected the less ornate "Lower" Barracks, home to the Royal Hampshire Regiment. Lower Barracks, having been disused for considerably longer than Upper Barracks, are in a worse state of decay. Both sets of buildings were marketed with outline planning permission for residential conversion six years ago but the buildings still await a buyer who will offer them a new use.

Short Block, Upper Barracks

Short Block, standing at the head of the U shaped upper barracks, was converted as a military museum. It now houses the museums of four regiments. Besides the Weapons Training shed which is used as a store and the Guard room, which continues to serve its original purpose, the other listed buildings: Long Block, Naffi Block, the 1856 Military Hospital (Mons Block) and the Chapel and Schoolroom, all stand empty, decaying.

Peninsular Barracks occupy an enviable position overlooking Winchester Cathedral. They have boundless potential and the local council are keen to find them a new use - there is demand for a new hotel in Winchester and these buildings might adapt perfectly.

BRUNEL'S BLOCKMILLS, PORTSMOUTH HARBOUR

Marc Brunel, father of the celebrated Isambard, was a Frenchman who had fled the revolution for America, becoming New York's City Engineer. There he developed a series of innovative machines for making ships' blocks. His marriage in 1801 to Sophia Kingdom, who was sister of the under-secretary to the British Navy Board, bryugh him to England where his invention revolutionised the Navy's shipbuilding programme.

At this time the Navy's requirement for wooden blocks (wheel shaped blacks of wood which take the strain on pulleys) was so great that the labour force simply could not cope with the demand. Brunel's 45 steam driven machines, completed in 1809, were able to produce 160,000 blocks a year, increasing production by over ten times. Portsmouth's Blockmills, which gave the navy a distinct advantage over her enemies, soon became a tourist attraction for industrialists.

The building housing the block making machines was designed by Brigadier-General Sir Samuel Bentham. It, and many of the machines, have survived to the present day. Though used until the 1960's for their original purpose, the buildings and machinery have since been left somewhat neglected and have fallen into a sorry state of repair. The navy are considering bringing the buildings back in to use, but it is hoped that they might hand them over to the care of the Portsmouth Naval Base Property Trust. Brunel's Blockmills are an exceptionally important relic of our industrial and naval heritage.

THE GRAND STORE HOUSE, HMS VERNON, PORTSMOUTH

The Grand Storehouse, conceived in an uncommonly monumental style for an ordnance building, was built in the latter years of the Napoleonic War. Its construction was commissioned by the Board of Ordnance, a separate Government department charged with responsibility for the military's guns and ammunition. The Board of Ordnance was abolished for inefficiency in 1855 and the site has since been in the hands of the Royal Navy. The grade II listed Grand Storehouse, otherwise known as the Vulcan Building, now forms part of the New Ordnance Wharf in the bounds of HMS Vernon.

Naval activity at HMS Vernon has been run down over the last few years and several of its historic buildings now stand redundant. The Grand Storehouse, disused for several years, is in a particularly sorry state. The MOD plan to dispose of HMS Vernon in the next few years and it urgently needs a new owner who will restore its historic buildings and put them to a suitable new use.

Though the core of the Eastney Barracks dates from 1862-8, the programme of building continued through till the reign of Edward VII. Built as the barracks of the Royal Marines Artillery, the site remained as a home of the Royal Marines until October 1991. Eastney Barracks is now on the market.

In 1983 the northern half of the Eastney Barracks site was sold off. Several late Victorian military buildings, including a number of barrack blocks and the Divisional School, were demolished in the ensuing redevelopment of the site as a housing estate. However, the vast majority of the important military buildings, in the southern half of the site, have been remarkably little altered and survive in good condition. Though the Royal Marines continue to use the Officers' Mess as a museum, other listed buildings, such as the Barracks on Gunners Walk and the Officers' Quarters on Tea Pot Row, have stood empty since the corps departed. They urgently need a new use. The 25 acre site, divided in to four lots, is being marketed for the MOD by Herring Baker Harris (071-734 8155).

Officers' Mess

The Officers' Quarters, Tea Pot Row

Barracks, interior, Gunners' Walk

The road that leads eastwards from Eastney Barracks to the South Eastern tip of Portsea Island is called Fort Cumberland Road. However the design of Cumberland fort, which lies but fifty yards from the road, is such that it lies well hidden. But take the Channel Islands plane from Southampton and the full extent of this magnificent Fort, arguably the finest eighteenth century defence structure in England, can be clearly seen.

The regularly planned brick faced pentagonal Fort was built in the 1760's on the site of an outmoded 1740's fort. Enclosing 24 acres with accommodation for 23 officers and 701 men, Fort Cumberland was the last self-contained fully bastioned fortress to be built in England. It has survived to this day in remarkably complete condition. Used by the Royal Marines as a training base until 1973, it is now in the guardianship of English Heritage whose archaeological team, the Central Excavations Unit have been resident there for some years. However the Fort, widely regarded as an historic military and architectural gem, has never been opened to the public. It may, however, pass into the care of Hampshire County Council and it is to be hoped that access will then be possible.

Part of the Granary

A quadrangle of single storey Cooperage buildings, dating from the 1760's, are the earliest buildings in Royal Clarence Victualling Yard. Other structures of the eighteenth century victualling operations on the site, previously known as Weevil Yard, were demolished in the building of the new yard from 1828-32. Comprising a formal entranceway, slaughterhouse, mill, granary and bakery, the new yard, named after the Lord High Admiral, the Duke of Clarence, was designed by G L Taylor, civil architect to the Navy Board. Though badly damaged by bombing during the second World War, most of the historic buildings have survived to this day.

Naval victualling operations at Clarence Yard have been wound down over recent years, its buildings now only have minimal storage use. There are plans to release part of the site in the near future. The historic buildings of Royal Clarence Victualling Yard are currently in good order: they will soon need a suitable new use to ensure their long term future.

Slaughterhouse and Cooperage

Priddy's Hard stands on a peninsular be tween Portsmouth Harbour and Forton Lake. Its isolated location made it a suitably safe place to store munitions and between 1769 and 1773 several magazines and ancillary buildings were erected on the site.

Priddy's Hard remained in naval use until 1989. The site, which comprises 110 acres, has since been put on the market. Gosport City Council are currently finalising the purchase of the historic South East corner of the site. While the rest of the area is due to be developed for housing, the council intend to preserve their 26 acres, which contain six out of Priddy's Hard's seven listed buildings, as a "heritage area". The site's museum will be opened up to the general public and its other historic structures restored and maintained. The rest of the "heritage area" will be sensitively re-developed.

The Gunboat Yard was designed and built in the mid nineteenth century by Scamp, a senior civil engineer with the navy. It is believed that a model of the Yard was shown at the Great Exhibition in 1851. Built for the refitting of small warships, the Yard comprised 10 covered repair sheds and 100 storage bays served by a single slipway. A steam driven traverser known as the elephant, approximately 42 metres long and capable of moving boats of up to 160 tons, shunted vessels across the yard.

In 1952 the Yard was refitted with a new slipway and an electrically operated transporter. By the early 1970's it was launching approximately 75 vessels per annum with an average refitting time of six weeks. However the erection of the Haslar Bridge in 1978 severely restricted the size of vessels sailing up to Haslar Yard and it was soon closed down. Since closure parts of the Yard have been demolished, but much of the site has been left untouched, it remains disused and derelict. It is not known what future plans the MOD have for the historic site.

Though there are currently no listed buildings on the site of HMS Daedalus, there are certainly some that are eminently worthy of consideration, for example the pre Second World War hangars and the imposing Lutyens Officers' Mess. HMS Daedalus, once the headquarters of the Fleet Air Arm, is now rarely used as a flying base and military activity on the site has been greatly reduced. It is hoped that the more important historic buildings on the site will have been protected by listing at the time of its release by the MOD next year.

ST GEORGE BARRACKS, MUMBY ROAD, GOSPORT

St George Barracks were built from 1856-59 on a site behind the northern extension of the late eighteenth century Gosport Lines. Sunken into the ground, they were designed with flat roofs and high parapets for an earth covering. Though Pevsner suggests that these quirks in design were due to the fact that the buildings were meant to be erected in the far east, it is more probable that they were designed as such for protection against bombardment.

The historic barracks now form two sections, split by Mumby Road. The grade II listed buildings north of the road have been unoccupied for two years and are now in a sorry state of repair. Those south of the road, still occupied on a temporary basis, have fared better. The whole site is due for release by the MOD shortly.

Fort Elson, constructed between 1855-60, stands at the Northern end of the line of polygonal forts built to defend the Western approach to Portsmouth. Disarmed in 1901, the Fort's use during the Second World War, as a depot for storing torpedoes and depth charges, led to its full time use as a Royal Naval Armaments Depot. The site has grown and the Fort, now no longer used (exept as a small arms range), has been left derelict. It is largely overgrown with saplings and brambles. Though attempts have been made to clear the moat, the Fort needs urgent attention to stem the tide of decay. However, Fort Elson's situation within the perimeter of the Armaments Depot means that release is unlikely: its future is in serious doubt.

Fort Rowner was built from 1859-62 as part of the fort building scheme to protect Portsmouth Harbour from an attack from the west. Designed by William Crossman, the polygonal fort, which featured a circular keep, was built, like its neighbouring forts, to house no less than seventy three guns. Rowner, which had barrack accommodation for three hundred men, was in fact used for much of the nineteenth century as an army barracks but has in recent years been left to fall into a sorry state of repair. The Palmerston Forts Society "Fortlog" describes the Fort thus: "The keep and flanking casemates are largely derelict. The ramparts are heavily overgrown with mature trees and impenetrable undergrowth. Part of the southern side of the moat has been infilled and a new entrance cut through the ramparts". Fort Rowner's unfortunate situation within the boundary of HMS Sultan means that its disposal by the MOD is unlikely. Its future looks bleak.

Fort Rowner's sister fort, Fort Grange, also designed by William Crossman, was completed in 1863. Likewise it was used as a barracks during the Victorian period. In 1914 the Fort was taken over by the Royal Flying Corps for use as a base for the nearby Grange airfield. Fort Grange remained in such use with the RAF until 1946, and with the British Helicopter Squadron for a further decade. In 1956, with Fort Rowner, it was incorporated into HMS Sultan. The Engineers' training establishment still uses the Fort for exercises. Though the MOD have recently carried out repairs to the fort, it remains in a very run down condition.

BREAKWATER FORT, WEYMOUTH

The Verne Citadel, Nothe Fort and Breakwater Fort were built to defend the new Portland Dockyard, constructed from 1860-72. Breakwater Fort, completely detached from the land, was built under civilian contract, using prison labour. The Fort's twelve 12'5" rifled muzzle loading cannon never saw active service and after the Second World War it was bricked up for protection against the weather. The Fort remains in the hands of the navy and is occasionally used for exercises. However though the breakwater has recently been repaired, the defence structures continue to deteriorate. The recent announcement that the Portland Naval Base will close down in 1996 adds further uncertainty to the Fort's future prospects.

C MAGAZINE, MARCHWOOD, HAMPSHIRE

Besides the significant loss of B Magazine through demolition, the early nineteenth century Royal Naval Armaments Depot is remarkably complete. That being said, practically all of the surviving buildings, now listed grade II, have stood empty and disused for many years and are in a sorry condition. However, Marchwood Yacht Club who have already restored the two gatehouses are looking to convert A Magazine and the Receiving Rooms to use as a clubhouse and interpretation centre.

C Magazine and the nearby examination rooms have a less certain future. Temporary repairs, carried out in 1988 as a result of local council enforcement action, are beginning to fail and they are in desperate need of restoration. The buildings, now in the hands of the receivers, are available for purchase. C Magazine, with its large open interior, would be well suited to conversion to office use.

HIGHER BARRACKS, EXETER

The Main Building

Higher Barracks, formerly known as Cavalry Barracks, dates from two builds of 1792 and 1867. Though they have continued in military use to the present day, latterly its buildings have only been partially occupied. It has recently been announced that the Army Pay Corps, and the other military welfare groups that currently use the buildings, will shortly be transferred to other sites. Higher Barracks is to be put on the market.

The 1867 married quarters, sold some time ago to the local council, are now threatened with demolition. Plans to level the historic buildings and build houses on their site are currently under discussion.

The Former Stables

THE ROYAL WILLIAM YARD, STONEHOUSE, PLYMOUTH

Constructed to the designs of the young Sir John Rennie, from 1825-33, the Royal William Victualling Yard forms the most impressive group of buildings in Plymouth and is one of the most important legacies of our naval heritage. The fourteen acre site, built at the end of the Cremyll Peninsula is described thus by Pevsner in the Buildings of England

"The first and most grandiloquent of the monumental compositions created by the Victualling Board of the Navy after the Napoleonic wars, the Yard is also among the most remarkable examples of an early c19 planned layout of industrial buildings anywhere in England."

Built of local limestone and dressed with ashlar, the magnificent buildings are topped and tailed with cornices and plinths of Cornish granite. Besides storehouses, in the complex were a bakery and flour mill, a brewery, a cooperage, a slaughterhouse and numerous other ancillary buildings. An ancient monument, the Yard boasts no less than seven grade I listed buildings.

Royal William Victualling Yard remained in Naval use until 1990. The decision to discontinue using the Yard came after a costings estimate, for the restoration of the run down buildings, had found against their retention. The buildings have since stood empty and disused.

Still in the hands of the MOD, the responsibility for the yard (and three other MOD sites) is soon to be handed over, with a large Government endowment, to the Plymouth Urban Development Corporation. All efforts must be made to find an appropriate and sympathetic new use.

Melville Square

The Mill House and Bakery

The Former Brewery

The Basin

ROYAL NAVAL HOSPITAL, STONEHOUSE, PLYMOUTH

The Stonehouse Naval Hospital was built from 1758-62 to the inventive designs of Alexander Rovehead. Laid out in axial lines, the series of buildings were designed to house a limited number of patients in each block so as to prevent contagion. They were the first of their type in England and their design was to prove extremely influential upon the French hospital reformers of the late eighteenth century. Situated by the (now blocked up) Stonehouse Creek, patients could be transferred directly from their ships to the hospital wards. Two further ranges of Edward Holl designed buildings were constructed on the site in the early nineteenth century.

Besides a small number of losses caused by the Second World War bombing raids, the historic hospital remains in remarkably complete order. Of its fifteen listed structures, two, Trafalgar Block and the Ward Blocks are listed grade II*. The possibility of its release from military service is currently being discussed by the MOD.

The 1860's casemates

Standing at the entrance of Plymouth Sound, Drakes Island has long been a strategically important defensive site. The island's military structures, which date from the early post medieval era through to the twentieth century, form an important microcosm of defence history. Amongst its most important structures are the early nineteenth century barrack block, the 1860's casemates and the batteries of the 1900's.

In the 1970's the MOD handed the island over to the control of the Crown Estate. It was then leased for several years to Plymouth City Council, who ran it as an adventure centre. Since their withdrawal in the mid 1980's the island has been largely disused. Though the Plymouth area Groundwork Trust have recently carried out much needed basic repairs to some of the structures, a full blown restoration scheme is long overdue.

The Barracks and Commanding Officer's house

The chain of five redoubts on Maker Hill were constructed at the request of the Duke of Richmond in 1782-3. The redoubts, which pre-date the Napoleonic conflict, are rare survivors of military structures built to defend against the American navy. But for Grenville Redoubt which saw military service through the First World War, the redoubts have been little used since their disarmament at the close of the Napoleonic wars in 1815.

Maker Barracks

Maker Barracks, dated 1804 are situated in the middle of the line of redoubts. Built in the second phase of defence construction, the barracks replaced temporary structures, housing personnel from the central three redoubts. Last used in 1989 as an educational facility for local schools, the barracks now stand empty: they are showing ominous signs of deterioration. It is not known what plans the Mount Edgecombe Estate, owners of the Barracks and the entire redoubt complex, have for their important, but decaying properties.

Tregantle Fort, the largest of Plymouth's land forts, dates from 1858-9. A scheduled ancient monument, it is owned by the MOD who continue to use the site as a rifle range. Its barracks, built to house a garrison of 2000 men, are still used by visiting regiments: they are in a good state of repair. However, the most unusual feature of the fort, the self contained keep, is in a worrying condition. Surplus to the needs of the military, it has stood empty for too long. The pitch on the roof has gradually perished and the resulting water penetration has caused damage to the interior panelling and woodwork. It is hoped that recent consultations between English Heritage and the military authorities responsible for the upkeep of the fort, will result in long overdue repairs.

Scraesdon, a sister fort to Tregantle, was built in 1860. It stands on a bluff overlooking the St Germans River, the northern most fort of the Antony Line. Though the military still use the fort, their interests lie principally in its elaborate network of tunnels which are much used for subterranean warfare exercises. As at Tregantle, the preservation of the fort's historic structure has principally been restricted to the areas that continue to serve a function. Vegetation grows rampant on the casemates, in places the stones are being wedged apart by the roots of sizeable trees. Water is causing serious damage to the interiors, particularly in the barracks, and much of the ironwork is also in urgent need of repair. The process of decay will accelerate for as long as the bushes and trees are allowed to run riot and action is urgently required.

A large defendable mobilisation depot was built in Bodmin in the late 1850's for the Royal Cornwall Militia. Ironically, considering the threat from France at that time, the building, listed grade II and known as the Keep, has a distinctly French Renaissance style.

In 1878 the depot was purchased by the War Department as part of the Cardwell Reforms. The 32nd and 46th foot became the first and second batallions of the Duke of Cornwall's Light Infantry and the depot was substantially enlarged. The barracks were in continuous use until 1959 when the Duke of Cornwall's Light Infantry merged with the Somerset Light Infantry. Within a matter of two years all but the keep had been abandoned.

The fortunes of each of the buildings on the site have varied, all have suffered through disuse, most through dereliction and some, demolition. The Married Quarters soon became vandalised to such an extent that the local council was forced to proceed with their demolition. The Barrack Block and the Sergeants Mess, which stood empty for many years are now used as warehouses by a large printing company whose offices and workshops litter the old parade ground. The rubblestone and granite dressed buildings are afforded scant respect and are gently crumbling. Similarly, the Old Hospital, now used as a nightclub is in a depressingly run down condition.

Encouragingly, the Officers' Mess and Quartermaster's and Commanding Officer's Houses are in pristine condition. Their owners, National Rivers Authority have recently carried out a thorough restoration programme. The Keep, which has always remained in the hands of the MOD, houses the Duke of Cornwalls Light infantry Museum and is used as the regional Light Infantry Office. It too is in a good state of repair.

The Barrack Block

The Old Hospital

The Officers Mess

Pembrock Dock and the Barracks to the right, from a nineteenth century watercolour celebrating the launch of the royal yacht, *Royal Sovereign*

The Royal Dockyard at Pembroke was founded in 1809 on a site across the Haven and transferred to the present site at Paterchurch Point in 1815. Within this fine natural harbour, halfway up the Haven estuary, the Dockyard was to become, by the middle of the nineteenth century, the navy's principal warship building yard.

Today, at less than one third of its previous size, the original layout has changed considerably: buildings have been demolished, nine of the fourteen magnificent building slips filled in or destroyed and many of the remaining Georgian offices and stores stand empty and disused.

In 1816 the first ship was launched, thereafter approximately two were built every year until 1850 when production increased to three or four. In 1817-18 the entrance to the Dockyard was built, and the massive limestone walls, subsequently strengthened and extended, enclosed the yard on the three landward sides. Officers' housing, a guard house and the Master's House were built at this time. In 1829 the naval yard at Deptford closed and men were transferred to Pembroke where facilities were increased accordingly. Many of the stores, offices and domestic buildings were designed by Edward Holl who was Civil Architect to the Admiralty from 1804-24.

The ship building slips - the finest in the country, with their ability to launch ships at all stages of the tide (and in 1858 the largest frigate in the world, Orlando) - were roofed over in 1845 with great iron structures, the work of engineers Fox & Henderson. Nothing remains of these today.

The navy remained at Pembroke throughout the nineteenth century until 1926 since when there has been a limited presence. In 1931 it became a base for the RAF with a number of seaplanes, and particularly the Sunderland Flying Boat, for which hangars were built - and still exist - in 1934. The RAF left in 1959 and much of the site was sold off to private enterprise, although the MoD still occupy a part, in particular the former Oakum Store which they use as offices.

The half of the dockyard containing many of the fine nineteenth century buildings, the chapel, the graving dock, remaining building slips and some interesting early sheds, belong to one individual, whose company, the Govan Davies Group, bought the dock with the intention of creating a major freight shipping port.

There is no doubt that Mr Davies has created much needed local employment; the local economy has benefitted and it is good to see activity at the docks again. However, the owner's intentions to expand his operations do not seem to provide for any of the historic buildings that his company owns and so far has had little regard for. Some are used as offices or have been crudely converted to flats, but others are standing empty and neglected. Windows are boarded up or smashed; roofs have slates missing and gutters blocked. Fine spear and tassel iron railings, where they still survive, have been allowed to rust. Piles of cut granite - coping stones and carved quoins - lie dumped, remnants of buildings and walls. One of the listed gate piers at the entrance to the dockyard was recently accidentally bashed by a heavy lorry.

Meanwhile, the offices of the Govan Davies Group are in a former early nineteenth century stores - reusing one of the old buildings, but modernised with new and inappropriate plastic windows.

The Irish boat continues to sail regularly to and from Pembroke bringing holiday traffic, and with the many tourists that visit Pembrokeshire every year, there must be opportunities that exist to reuse the Georgian buildings in the dockyard. A museum charting the history of this once great naval enclave, with its timber yards, pickling ponds and saw mills would surely be a popular attraction. It is a disgrace that the dockyard that served the nation well has been so badly treated and its precious historic fabric so rudely ignored.

DOCKYARD CHAPEL

George Ledwall Taylor, who was civic architect to the Navy Office designed the chapel in 1830. Whilst working for the navy he carried out a survey of all the naval docyards which is to be found in the National Maritime Museum at Greenwich. Standing at the western end of the dockyard, at the end of an overgrown avenue of trees, it is an elegant building and in type very rare in Wales. By 1989 the chapel had been long closed and neglected, lead stripped from the roof, windows broken, render crumbling. Govan Davies applied to demolish the chapel but met with fierce resistance and permission was refused. The chapel continues to decay despite being listed grade II.

These two buildings form a symmetrical composition either side of the main dockyard entrance. They were designed in 1817-18 by Edward Holl who was Civil Architect to the Admiralty from 1804-24. They must have once given a grand first impression on approaching the dockyard, through square stone piers flanked by low pavilions although one of the piers has been badly damaged by a heavy lorry, the handsome contemporary iron gates have long since disappeared and graffiti stains the stonework. One of the buildings is a hotel whilst the other has been made into flats.

One of the most interesting and important features of these buildings is their roof construction: the iron structure is believed to be the earliest of its kind in the country.

FORMER GUARDHOUSE

This dates from 1820's or 1830's and is built of stone with ashlar quoins and dressings. It is a square shaped building with projecting wings and a simple projecting portico with four stone columns over the round-headed doorway and windows. Like the Captain's house next door, it is empty and boarded up.

FORMER CAPTAIN SUPERINTENDENT'S OFFICE

Built in the 1820's or 1830's, this building is shown in 1858 as the Captain Superintendent's office. It was used as the RAF Post Office in the Second World War but now stands completely empty and neglected. Whilst its lower windows are boarded up, the ones above are blank gaping holes. Inside it is completely stripped although it still has its original railings. Standing on the main route through the dockyard it is continually passed by traffic, yet has been in this state for years.

There were two buildings like this, one was demolished in 1981. It was designed by Edward Holl and dates from between 1820 and 1831. It is built of rubble stone with quoins, cornice and parapet of granite. The long elevations have a central pediment and there was once a clock tower above. This building is a good example of Holl's cast iron building construction with iron columns and iron roof construction and is listed grade II* for this reason.

FORMER OFFICERS' HOUSING

Plans and drawings by Holl exist for this building, which stands in The Terrace in the Dockyard, dating from 1817-18. A most elegant pair of houses in ashlar with a slate roof and arched windows at ground level between arched doorways (one of which has been changed to a window). The building has been converted to a number of flats. Some of the original railings survives.

FORMER OFFICES

Dating from the middle of the nineteenth century, these are presently used as offices for Govan Davies. Note the modern windows - completely inappropriate in style.

THE DEFENCES OF PEMBROKE AND MILFORD HAVEN

By the 1850's the safety of the Pembroke Dock, together with other strategic sites in the south of England, had become an urgent priority. Existing defences were weak - little had been built in the way of fortifications since the reign of Henry VIII, and now not only was the protection of shipbuilding at the dockyard vital but also the anchorage of the Haven.

A series of forts were built, two on islands at the mouth of the estuary and two gun towers sited in shallow water either side of the dockyard. The Defensible Barracks were started in 1841, on high ground above the town of Pembroke.

The defences built at Pembroke and Milford Haven are a unique example of their kind. Milford Haven is one of the few defended ports in Britain where the fortifications are virtually all of one date, having been constructed during a 20 year period. And yet there is considerable difference in design and each fort has distinctive features. Although most have been disused and abandoned since the Second World War much of the original structure, stonework, brick vaulting, ironwork and steel shutters remain.

Their tremendous interest has been recognised by Pembrokeshire National Park, who are currently carrying out a detailed survey of all the fortifications in their area, with a view to creating a 'heritage trail' for visitors interested in military history.

HUBBERSTONE FORT

According to its grade II* listing description this major fort is comparable only with the contemporary defences of the Solent in Britain, and yet it is largely unknown and appears utterly abandoned. It was built in 1863-65 as a defensible barracks and gun battery with a capacity for 28 heavy guns and a garrison for 250 men.

Hubberstone is quite remarkable for the quality of its stone and brickwork. It stands on headland, just outside Milford Haven, and in an excellent position to command the entrance to the Haven. The two main elements of the fort, the barracks and the battery, on lower ground, have an area of scrubland between them, with steep paths through the gorse. Despite being very overgrown and daubed with extensive graffiti most of the original structure is still intact. It is a fascinating warren of tunnels, vaults, steep stone steps and massive granite framed gun openings with views to the sea beyond.

Two gun towers (East Martello and West Martello) were built in 1849-57 for the immediate protection of Pembroke Dockyard. They are on an unusually small scale with guns on top to command the inner walls. The towers housed sergeants of the artillery and their families but were vacated by the military in 1905 and have lain empty since. However, there are plans for their restoration - one is to be a local history museum.

POPTON FORT

Popton Fort is an important fort, one of the designs of Lt Col Drummond Jervois who became Deputy Director of Fortifications in the 1850's and was responsible for defences at Alderney and Portsmouth as well as Milford Haven. Popton Fort was built from 1859-64. It now lies within the large oil refinery.

WEST BLOCKHOUSE FORT

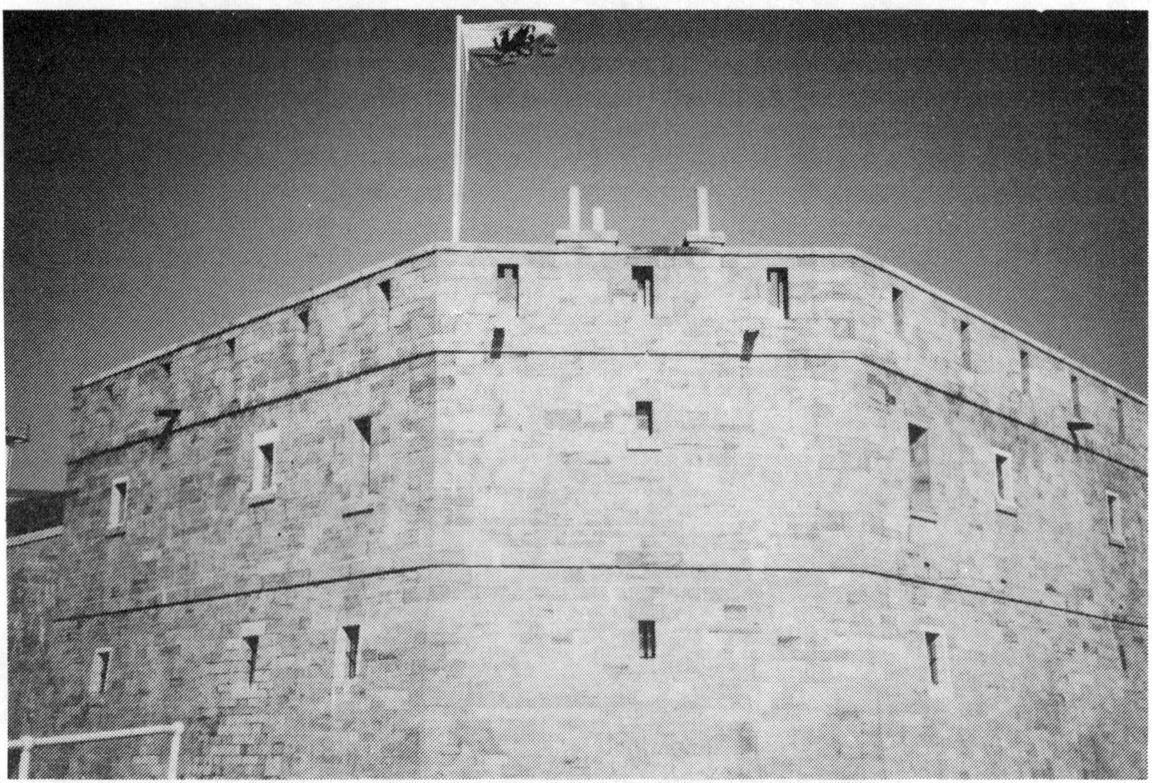

Built from 1852-57 and subsequently reinforced, the Fort was acquired by the Landmark Trust who let it out for short lets. It has been beautifully restored.

DEFENSIBLE BARRACKS 1841

Entrance to the Barracks, before conversion

An army garrison was considered necessary to defend the Dockyard, in addition to the naval garrison stationed there, and the Defensible Barracks were built in 1844-45 above the town. A walk across the bridge and in through the forbidding fortified gateway brings you into a delightful courtyard surrounded by attractive Georgian granite facades reminiscent of Edinburgh. In recent years the accommodation barracks fell into grave disrepair, however they have now been restored as houses and offices. The fortifications to the rear are decaying slowly but are still very much in evidence.

Accommodation Barracks

FORT SCOVESTON

Built as part of the landward defences, Fort Scoveston was a large octagonal structure, designed for up to 32 guns. It was started in 1859 when a series of similar defences were planned, but only Scoveston was carried out. Being sunken into rising ground inland from Milford Haven, it is hardly visible from the road, hidden by gorse and grazing sheep. Yet what remains is still of great interest.

STACK ROCK FORT

Work commenced on Stack Rock, an island at the mouth of the Haven, in 1850, but it was modified following the Royal Commission report. Of the two gun casemates originally planned, one was converted into barracks. As one of the most strategically placed of the sea batteries, Stack Rock Fort is a major landmark. Since its abandonment its location has saved it from being vandalised but the ironwork has been removed and it is now deteriorating very quickly.

SOUTH HOOK FORT

Also within the oil refinery, but on the north side of the Haven, South Hook was built 1859-65. Years after its desertion it still had its wooden floors and chimney pots but recently it has been badly vandalised.

DALE POINT BATTERY

This large, 12 gun battery (reinforced in the 1900's) has been converted to a field studies centre.

CHAPEL BAY BATTERY

An open battery of c1868, remodelled in 1900 and considerably altered before that.

THORN ISLAND FORT

Built in 1852, this nine gun battery was built on an island just of Angle point. These forts were carefully sited so that their cross fire could cover any ship entering the Haven.

NORTON BARRACKS, NORTON, WORCESTER

The recent history of Norton Barracks is very sad. Sold to developers with no interest beyond their pockets, the historic buildings have become victims of the recession.

Built as the home of the Worcestershire Regiment in 1877, the Barracks remained in army use for just over a century, being sold by the MOD in 1982. Through the 1980's the military buildings and their 45 acre site were passed from one speculating developer to the next. Though the condition of the Barracks worsened through decay, their speculative value. However, the proposed schemes were never implemented and the Barracks still stand empty. Their owner is planning an intensive development. After months of discussion with the local council, it seems likely that the current scheme will go ahead. The proposals are that bar the Keep, all of Norton Barracks, including the two barrack blocks flanking the parade ground, will be demolished. In their place will be erected about four hundred houses. The grade II listed Keep and its adjoining wings will be converted to about thirty flats.

J. Dugdale, in his 1819 publication British Traveller, attributes the Royal Naval Hospital, built 1809-11, to the official Naval architect of that time, Edward Holl. Others contend that it was designed by William Pilkington, pupil of Robert Taylor. Built of yellow brick with Portland stone dressings, the grade II* listed hospital, in Pevsner's words, has a composition that is "utilitarian" but is "remarkably monumental and ought to be better known".

Built at a time when the North Sea Fleet were based at Yarmouth, the new hospital was to treat the wounded shipped back from the Napoleonic Wars. The buildings were converted into barracks in 1818 and were used as such until the Crimean War, when they were re-fitted for hospital use and subsequently became a military lunatic asylum.

In the 1950's the hospital was turned over to civilian use, and has since been a NHS psychiatric hospital. However it has been gradually closing for several years and will shut completely in December 1993.

The Royal Naval Hospital is an extremely important example of military architecture. The buildings are remarkable in that, unlike their peers, they have been little altered by the regular changes imposed by different military requirements. Furthermore they are in a good state of repair. To find a suitable new use which will not compromise this historic legacy is of paramount importance.

The Royal Naval Hospital Chapel

SANDON ROAD BARRACKS, GRANTHAM

Sandon Road Barracks were built in the mid nineteenth century as the home of the Royal South Lincolnshire Militia. They remained in military service until the 1950's, being released by the MOD soon after the end of the Second World War. In County Council ownership the barracks were leased for several decades to Grantham College of Further Education. The ranges flanking the drill square were turned in to classrooms and the Keep used for storage. However, since the College's withdrawal from the site in the mid eighties, the buildings have stood empty and at risk from vandalism. They have recently been purchased by a developer who is seeking permission for an office conversion. The application is likely to be accepted. The adaptation of the almost windowless Keep will pose a more challenging problem.

DRILL HALL, POYSER STREET, WREXHAM

This turn of the century red brick drill hall stands empty, its owner contemplating its demolition. He could make substantial profits out of the redevelopment. Furthermore, the local council, their minds set on enhancing a strictly residential area, would condone such action if the site were to be used for housing.

Home to the Territorial Army, drill halls are rarely afforded the respect they deserve. These late Victorian and Edwardian structures are usually situated close to the town centre. On release by the army, there is often immense development pressure on the site, which in the past, has often resulted in demolition.

Though unashamedly utilitarian, the Poyser Street Drill Hall has architectural dignity. Buttresses, crenellations in shallow relief, stepped gables and arrow slits give the facade a distinctly military feel. Its glass roof bathes the interior with light. Since the army moved out in the late 1960's, the drill hall has been put to a number of uses, most recently as an auctioneers showroom. It clearly has the potential for adaption to a great variety of commercial or community uses. However, the fact remains, its future is very much in question.

ROWDITCH BARRACKS, UTTOXETER OLD ROAD, DERBY

The regimental amalgamations of Cardwell's reforms of the late 1870's brought about a spate of barrack building; in Derby, the new Normanton Barracks were built to house the recently coupled 45th and 95th regiments of foot. These radical changes rendered the Rowditch Barracks, built in 1859 to house Derbyshire Volunteer Rifle Corps, obsolete.

Upon closure, the buildings were taken over for use as a laundry, continuing until after the Second World War. Since then, in the hands of the local council, the accommodation blocks have been converted to houses for council workers and the drill square to tennis courts. However, the main barrack block, put to a low grade storage use has been gradually deteriorating. The council have been parsimonious in their maintenance: the building now suffers from both wet and dry rot and needs urgent attention to its ground floor ceiling. Rowditch Barracks, situated within a park but half a mile from the town centre, have enormous potential for a variety of high grade uses. Their current state is a shameful waste.

THE DRILL HALL, BRIDGE ROAD, MACCLESFIELD

A gothic machicolated tower looms above the roofs of Macclesfield's Drill Hall, designed presumably to overawe recruits. The Drill Hall was built in 1871 as a training centre for the Cheshire Militia. Latterly used by the TA, it was closed in 1990 and has since stood empty. Outline planning consent has recently been granted for the facade rooms to be converted to residential or office use and the huge metal framed hall to be used for a market. Though the building is in a reasonable state of repair, there are already signs of deterioration and it is hoped that the new use will be implemented as soon as possible.

FORT PERCH ROCK, NEW BRIGHTON, MERSEYSIDE

Fort Perch Rock was built to the designs of Captain J. Sykes Kitson RE from 1826-29. Defensive structures of this date are rare, as the main fort building initiative had ceased after the Napoleonic threat, and Palmerstone's extensive programme had not yet begun. Fort Perch Rock was in fact built to defend the prosperous port at Liverpool against the very real threat of American marauders. It remained in military use until the late 1950's, when, with the abolition of coastal artillery outfits, it became redundant. Having languished in disuse for many years, the building was taken on by a keen member of the Fortress Study Group who took strident action to restore the Fort to its late nineteenth century appearance. Parts of the structure were converted to housing and a museum was installed. However, Fort Perch Rock has been closed to the public for the last three years and there is mounting concern for its future.

Burniston Barracks, built originally in 1861 to house one hundred men of the artillery, were enlarged in the 1880's as a result of the Cardwell reforms. The barracks have had a chequered history, occupied by scores of different regiments and temporarily closed from 1918-19 and 1961-62. In 1992 The TA Royal Signals training unit vacated the barracks: this time, they will not be re-occupied. The site is now being marketed with planning consent for a housing redevelopment. Attempts to get the historic buildings listed have thus far been turned down: their fate lies in the hands of the developers.

FENHAM BARRACKS, NEWCASTLE UPON TYNE

Very little survives of the Fenham Barracks. In the mid 1970's when the army abandoned the site the bulldozers moved in and only four historic buildings escaped demolition. Though all four early nineteenth century buildings are now listed, their futures remain uncertain. O and P Blocks, the former barracks, are built in English bond brick. They have stood empty for too long and they are in an appalling state. While the O block suffers from dry rot, P block, gutted by fire five years ago, is roofless and now covered by scaffolding and polythene. Both have planning permission and listed building consent for conversion to student accommodation and it is hoped that Newcastle University will take this up in the near future.

The two entrance lodges, listed grade II* have fared slightly better. After the departure of the military they were converted to use as a pub and restaurant. However for the last couple of years they have both stood empty and disused. Their owner has gained planning permission for office use. The single storeyed sandstone lodges, thought to be by James Wyatt in 1806, are currently on the market.

P Block, Fenham Barracks

FORT CLARENCE, BORSTAL ROAD, ROCHESTER

Fort Clarence, part of the advanced Napoleonic defences, was given the dual role of protecting Chatham Dockyard and Rochester Bridge. Built in 1812 of stock brick, with limestone dressings, the three storey turreted fort has a distinctly medieval look about it. Now listed grade II and in the ownership of British Telecom, the fort stands empty and deteriorating, its future in question.

MARTELLO NO 28, RYE HARBOUR

The ravages of the weather and a general lack of repairs have caused martello No 28 to suffer. Its render is crumbling and a carpet of ivy has begun to envelop the exposed brickwork of this circular structure.

However, No 28, erected in 1806 as a defence against the perceived French invasion, was built to last. Its six to twelve foot thick walls were constructed of brick bonded by hot lime mortar, a mix of lime, ash and hot tallow that set "like iron". It would take literally hundreds of years for its structure to crumble.

In the late 1980's the future of Rye Harbour Martello No 28 looked promising. Both scheduled monument consent and planning permission were granted for its conversion to residential use. However, the conditions of purchase proved a stumbling block and the scheme was never carried out.

The site of the martello is compromised by the close proximity of a caravan park. Its most suitable future use might be as a museum or "interpretation centre" for either the historic Rye coastal defences, or the Rye Harbour Nature Reserve.

CHRISTCHURCH BARRACKS, DORSET

The oldest buildings at Christchurch Barracks, dating from 1795, were built as part of the nations first organised programme of barrack building. Most imposing of these is the grade II listed nine bayed brick barrack block, whose ground floor was designed for stabling. Though built for the cavalry, the barracks later became home to the Royal Artillery and the Royal Engineers. Cardwells Reforms gave rise to a second building programme in the 1870's. In recent times Christchurch Barracks have been used as a military vehicule experimental establishment. Sadly the late eighteenth century barrack block, surplus to modern military requirements, has fallen in to a sorry state of repair. The MOD's decision to close down and market Christchurch Barracks, places a further question mark over its, and the rest of the site's future.

LEICESTER PARADE, NORTHAMPTON

These late eighteenth century buildings on Leicester Parade were originally part of an extensive military complex built as the depot of the 48th Regimental District. Approximately two thirds of the site was sold by the MOD to the Post Office in 1980 and has subsequently been redeveloped as a sorting office. Leicester Parade, and other surviving military buildings dating from a later 1880's build, have stood empty and disused for many years. However, within the last year they have been sold by the MOD to the East Midlands Housing Trust. Their conversion to residential use is now underway.

THE HOUNSLOW CAVALRY BARRACKS

The Hounslow Barracks are amongst the finest historic military buildings currently in the army's use. Thankfully the military authorities implementing the building programmes of the mid nineteenth century and 1870's resisted the temptation to start afresh and the 1790's buildings, designed by James Johnson, have survived in remarkably complete order. However, Hounslow Barracks are due for disposal by the MOD. The future of the many grade II listed buildings will again be put in jeopardy.

No 12, TEA CADDY ROW, RMA SANDHURST

The line of twelve attractive yellow stock brick houses, quaintly known as Tea Caddy Row, date from the early nineteenth century. It is not known why one of the twelve has been permitted to fall into a perilous state of decay. Thirty years of dereliction have given rise to severe problems, most particularly with rot in the roof timbers and flooding in the basement. The feasibility study, currently being carried out by the Property Services Agency and the MOD, is long overdue.

COLLIERGATE DRILL HALL, YORK

In 1872 Gould & Fisher were commissioned to build a "drill shed" in the heart of the city. The architects, best known for their ecclesiastic work, designed a building with buttresses and gothic windows which could quite easily be mistaken for a church or chapel. The drill shed saw continuous use as a training centre for the York Rifle Volunteers and more recently the T.A, until Autumn 1992. It is about to be put on the market. The building has outline planning consent for office use and is currently being considered for listing. Hopefully a good scheme of conversion will come forward.

JELLALABAD BARRACKS, TAUNTON

This red brick Cardmore barracks was built in 1879 to replace a smaller late eighteenth century barracks. Though nothing exists of the Georgian buildings, the barracks, called Jellalabad after the Somersetshire Light Infantry's most famous battle honour, survive in their entirety.

DEMOLISHED

KNIGHTSBRIDGE BARRACKS

The Georgian Knightsbridge barracks, built in 1779, survived for exactly a century. An article in the Household Brigade Magazine at the time of its demolition, reports that a deputation at the War Office urged demolition. According to the Right Hon. Robert Lowe, M.P, "There was not a shabbier, uglier, or more unsightly building in the metropolis."

The Georgian Barracks

On the opening of the new barracks in 1880, the Household Brigade Magazine praised the new barracks, saying, "For architectural features, sanitary arrangements, and commodiousness it is said to be the finest in Europe, and certainly in advance of anything of the kind attempted in any part of the United Kingdom."

The Victorian Knightsbridge barracks failed, by over a decade, to reach their centenary: they were demolished in 1969. The Household Brigade Magazine declared the buildings "in every way unsuitable for their purpose, and altogether behind the times." The replacement barracks, designed by Sir Basil Spence, were completed in 1972. At that time they too were acclaimed as an architectural masterpiece. However, the building hasn't proven to be as efficient as expected and there are already maintenance worries. How long will the Spence building last before the Household Brigade Magazine, in time honoured tradition, writes its scathing condemnation for another state of the art, hard working, but tired building?

The Dining Room, Officers' Mess in the Victorian Barracks

The Officers' Mess, Victorian Barracks

The Stable Yard

The Wellington Barracks, the headquarters of the five regiments of Foot Guards, stand within a stone's throw of Buckingham Palace. Its buildings, as well as serving a utilitarian purpose, play their part in the ceremonial duties of the Guards. Since their erection in the 1830's, the Grecian style barracks have stood as a classical backdrop to the mounting of the guard.

In the late 1960's the run-down appearance of the Wellington Barracks gave rise to angry complaints which, in due course, led to their inspection by a Government minister. The full extent of the decay was shocking, besides peeling stucco work and internal rot there were obvious signs of subsidence.

The recommendation of the consultant architects, George, Trew, Dunn, was that the central barrack block and its wings (the so called facade buildings) should be levelled and replaced by new barracks. The advice, stiffly opposed from many fronts, was thankfully cast aside and the architects were commissioned to put forward a scheme involving the retention of the main frontages.

The resulting restoration cum conversion, delayed by changes in Government, was eventually completed in 1986. Subsidence, the primary threat to the future of grade II listed barracks, was remedied by underpinning. While the interiors were totally gutted and replaced, the facade was restored to its its original splendour. The Wellington Barracks facade buildings now house military offices and archives.

The late 1960's saw the demolition of numerous historic military buildings. The Wellington Barracks, presumably due to their high public profile, were spared the fate of their peers. They stand as remarkable survivors of an uncompromising era.

CHELSEA BARRACKS

The "new" Guards Barracks, built to accommodate 1,000 soldiers was completed in 1861. The building, which stretched a quarter of a mile along the road leading to a new suspension bridge, were acknowledged in the Guards Magazine of 1863 as "the most convenient, and in all respects the most perfect for their size in the kingdom". However, within less than a decade, enthusiasm for the buildings had waned considerably. The Guards Magazine of 1868 reports that the construction of the barrack rooms left "nothing to desire" and that the dark and ojectionable lavatories were imperfectly ventilated, their foul air entering the passages and barrack rooms. Furthermore it appears that the architect was no rifleman: the basement, designed as a rifle range, had to be used for storage, "since it was found impossible to shoot from end to end for want of height for the trajectory".

All that remains of the old barracks now are the church and the railings that surround the site. They were demolished in their centenary year, 1961; few tears were shed at their loss. The replacement barracks, completed in 1962 were described at the time, in an article written by Lieutenant J.B. Blackett for the Guards Magazine, as "the finest and most modern barracks in England's military world" a "precast concrete utopia"!

The Entrance, Chelsea Barracks

The Kensington Cavalry Barracks, built close by Kensington Palace, were designed by Colonel Frederick Chapman. Construction began in the 1840's, and though largely completed by 1857, the barracks were still being added to in 1869, when the looming 278 foot high spire of the nearby Gilbert Scott church, St Mary Abbot's, was completed. The Barracks remained in military use until 1972, but within ten years of closure were demolished. In the shadow of Gilbert Scott's spire now stands a shopping mall.

Records suggest that Warley Common was used as a regular military training camp as early as 1742. In 1804 it became a permanent military station and was taken over in 1843 by the East India Company as a training centre for recruits. After the Indian Mutiny of 1857, the depot was returned to regular army use. Since the Cardwell Reforms of the late 1870's the barracks have been inexorably associated with the Essex Regiment.

The reductions in the armed forces of the late 1950's brought about the sale and subsequent demolition of the Warley Barracks. Though little or nothing had survived from the earliest days of the barracks, the bulldozers cleared both the barracks erected by the East India Company and late nineteenth century buildings. The site was purchased by Ford for their U.K headquarters; by the mid 1960's they had erected a nine storey tower block where the barracks had once stood. Cowering in its shadow are the only survivors of the development, the 1857 Regimental Chapel and the slightly later Headquarters Building. Both are now listed grade II. Though they were given a stay of execution by the return of the T.A to Warley in 1986, the future of the buildings is uncertain.

Warley Barracks during demolition

The only survivor of Ipswich's old barracks is a wall that stands in the grounds of a hospital just north of the city centre. Records of the old barracks are scarce but it is known that the Cavalry Barracks on Barrack lane, were built in the 1790's and that the Artillery Barracks on Anglesea Road were probably of the same date. Both were taken out of military use in 1929 and within three years the Artillery Barracks were demolished. The Cavalry Barracks, despite being converted for housing, subsequently met the same fate.

These red brick and stone dressed Cardwell Barracks were built in 1878 for the Suffolk Regiment. They saw constant military use until 1960 when, following the amalgamation of the Suffolk Regiment into the East Anglian Regiment, they were vacated. All of the buildings on this large complex, bar the Keep, were subsequently demolished to be replaced by a sports centre, a college and a car park. The Keep has been turned into use as the museum of the Suffolk Regiment.

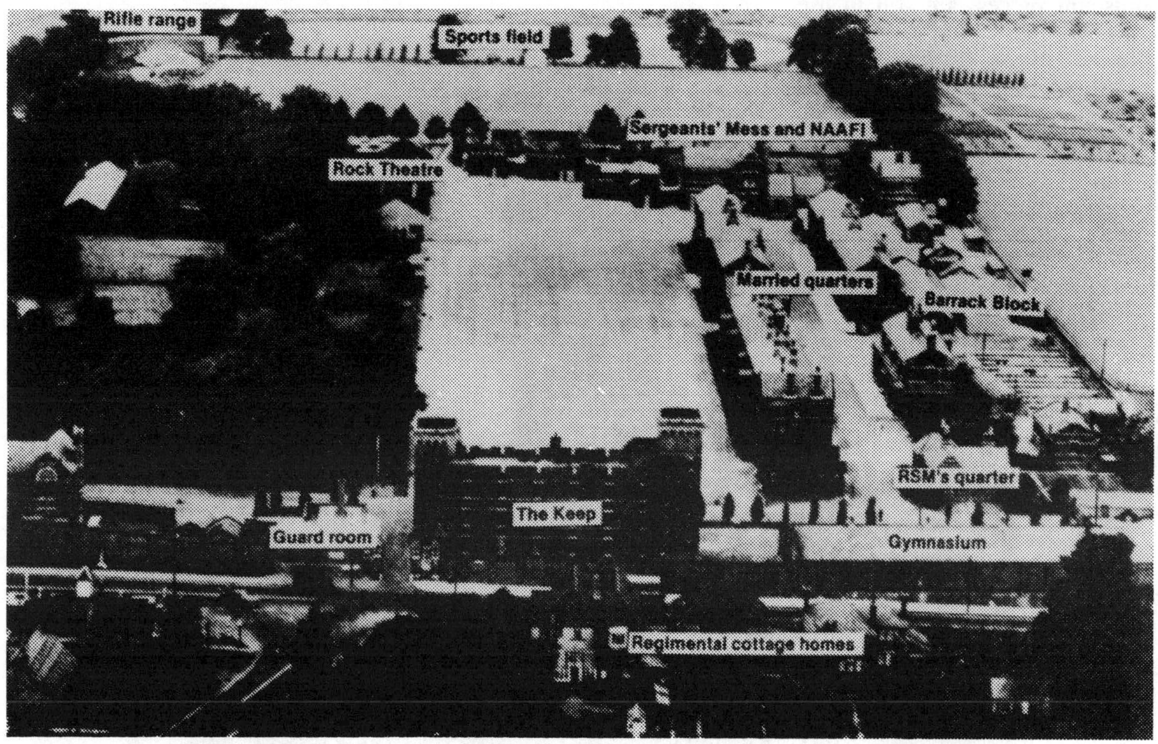

In 1812 John Rennie (the elder) was commissioned to re-design the mid seventeenth century dockyard at Sheerness. Though much of the dockyard was completed by his death in 1821, further buildings were erected over the following decade under the charge of the official naval architects, Edward Holl and his pupil George Taylor. It stands as a tribute to its designers that while in naval use, the Dockyard was remarkably little altered. However, since its disposal in 1960, the Docks have undergone considerable change and many of the historic buildings have been lost. But Sheerness Dockyard, now run by the Medway Ports Authority, continues to serve its original purpose and most of its surviving historic structures, rather than being mothballed or dressed as museum pieces, are still in use.

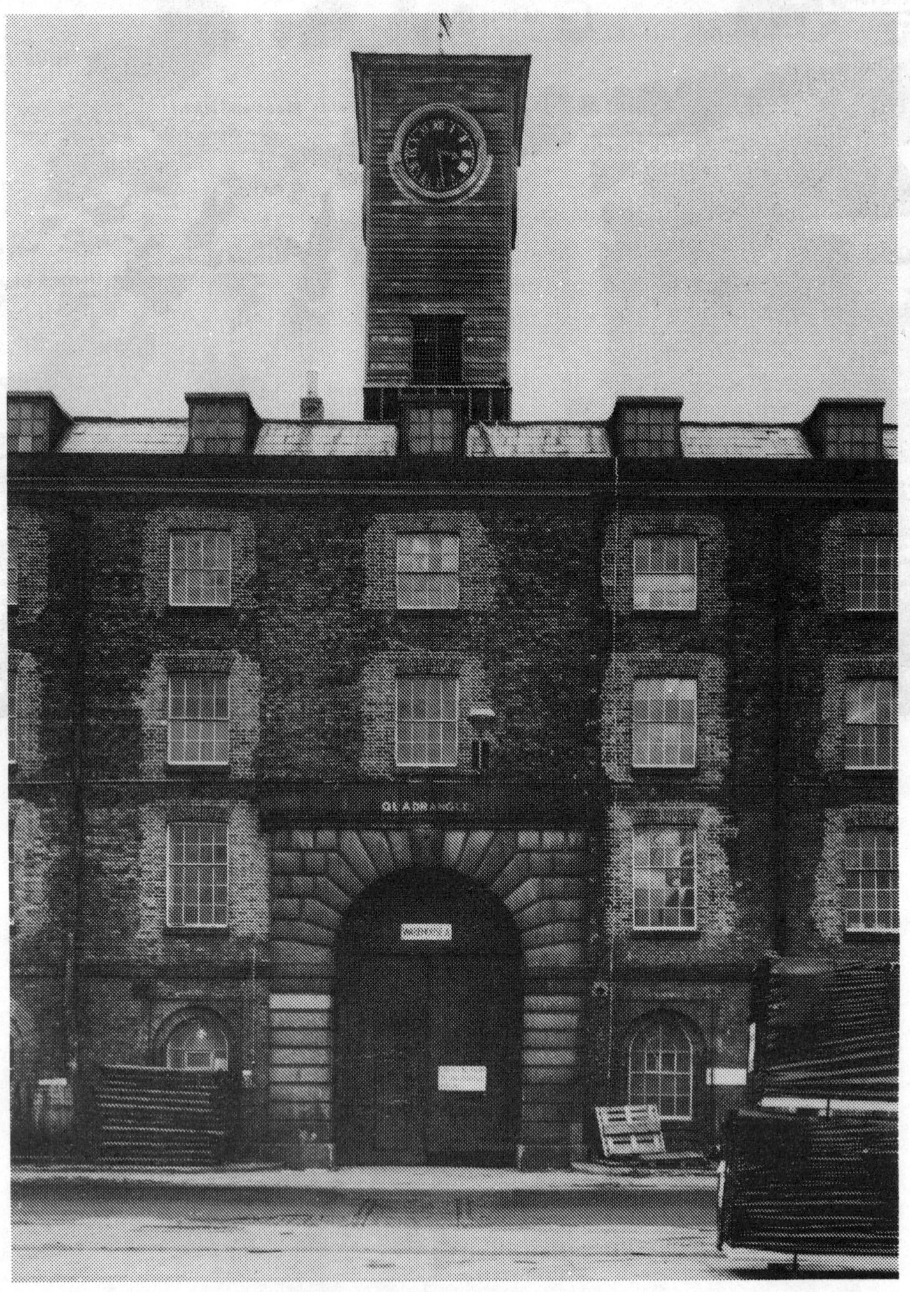

THE GREAT QUADRANGLE STOREHOUSE BUILDING

The centrepiece of Rennie's Dockyard was an enormous four floored storehouse whose ranges were built around a quadrangle. Built to Holl's designs from 1824-9, it had sturdy stock brick walls and imposing rusticated granite entrance archways. However by the mid 70's the building, deemed unsuitable for modern use and a waste of valuable storage area, was demolished. It had only recently received a grade II* listing. A deplorable loss.

RENNIE'S DRY DOCKS

Of the five 1820's dry docks built to Rennie's designs, only two remain in use. No's 1,2 and 3 have been filled in with sand to create further storage space, whilst 4 and 5 are used by the Medway Dry Docks Company for their original purpose.

THE BOAT STORE

The grade II* listed Boat Store, built in 1859 to the designs of Col G.T Green, is of paramount architectural significance. The destruction of the first South Kensington Museum and Crystal Palace has led to this building's unrivalled claim to be the earliest surviving example of a rectilinear iron-framed structure. It is built with simple H-section cast iron columns and beams.

Thankfully this important building has escaped demolition. Considered structurally unsuitable for storage purposes, it has languished in minimal use for many years. Now only the ground floor is used as storage space for "timber and forest products". The architectural and historic importance of the Boat Store should not be underestimated: its distinctly down at heel appearance and questionable future are of national concern.

THE GARRISON CHURCH

The original 1828 George Taylor church was destroyed by fire. Its replacement, which incorporated the original clock tower, was built in 1884. Though the late victorian church has been spared fire and the bulldozers, it too has had an unfortunate recent history. After the Naval withdrawal the grade II listed building was converted to a squash court. That use has since ceased and it is now used for storage. The decay of the fabric has been exacerbated by lack of adequate maintenance and subsidence problems. The Sheerness Fort and Dockyard Installation Group have recently expressed an interest in the church with regard to its conversion to a museum. It would make an eminently suitable showcase for the Rennie Model of Sheerness Dock which is currently gathering dust in package cases far from public view.

This Royal Commission fort, armed with rifled muzzle-loaders, was built in the 1860's to defend the entrance to the Medway River. The unusual D shaped fortified keep, which used its two tiers of casemates for accommodation, was surrounded by earth ramparts housing magazines and firing positions. Though, as with all defensive structures of this date its capability of repelling attackers was never put to the test, it would have proved an awkward obstacle for any would be invader.

Grain Fort saw its first and only active use in the Second World War. Abandoned by the military in 1956, it had a slow death, being demolished piece-meal over the course of a decade. The site upon which the fort once stood is now a grassed over recreation area.

In 1777 a site to the south of the Chatham Dockyard was purchased for the erection of barracks for the Royal Marines. The buildings constructed over the following decade show marked similarities with the slightly later Royal Marine barrack buildings at Deal. As at Deal, the early barracks were supplemented by a further building programme of the late nineteenth century. Chatham Barracks were abandoned by the Marines in 1950 and after about twenty five years in use as a paper store, they were demolished. The site where they once stood is now occupied by a Lloyds of London office.

St Mary's Barracks were built from 1807-12 at the North Eastern end of the Chatham Lines. Built to accommodate infantrymen but used during the Napoleonic War to house French prisoners, the Barracks were later put to a great variety of uses other than that for which they were intended, namely as a married quarters, a powder magazine and a balloon factory. This century they were occupied as barracks until their demolition in 1960.

The Chatham Lines, a partially bricked earthwork defensive ditch built in the 1790's to defend Chatham from landward offensives, is still largely intact. Fort Amherst, standing at the South Western end of the Lines, is a remarkable example of an unaltered, well preserved mid eighteenth century fort in the hands of a specially formed trust. It is well worth a visit.

Building work on Fort Bridgewoods was started at the same time as its neighbour, Fort Borstal, but funding for the fort building programme dried up soon after the completion of Fort Borstal in 1883. The enthusiasm to complete Fort Bridgewoods dwindled as rapid development in artillery at this time led to doubts as to the effectiveness of the ring forts and the threat of invasion had waned. It was only the renewed fear of war that led to Fort Bridgewood's completion in 1892.

In 1980 Fort Bridgewoods, then owned by Kent County Council, was destroyed to make way for a commercial development.

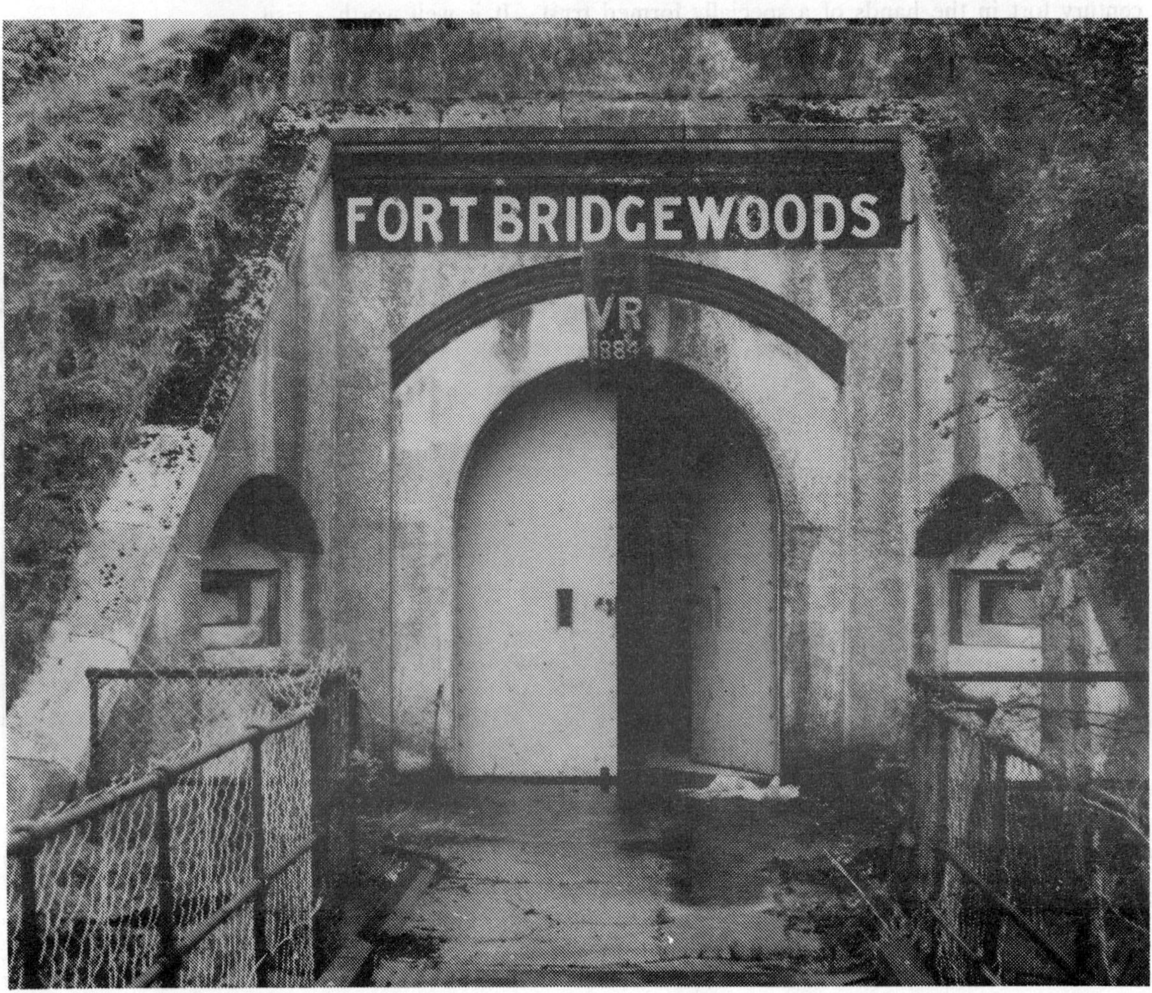

The Hythe School of Infantry was set up in 1809 in response to the threat of a Napoleonic invasion. The depot, which was turned into a school of musketry in 1853, remained in military use until 1969. Upon closure, the buildings were left to rot. Their demise did not go unnoticed and in 1973 the Hythe Civic Society launched a spirited campaign for their preservation. However, despite the society's success in getting the buildings listed, the threat remained. The South Eastern Electricity Board had already secured planning permission to redevelop the site and applied for listed building consent to demolish. The public inquiry found against the historic buildings and in 1975, European Architectural Heritage Year, the school of infantry was demolished. In its place the South Eastern Electricity Board erected offices and a distribution depot.

Though the first major phase of barrack building came as a result of Cardwell's reforms of the 1870's, there had been an earlier spate at the end of the eighteenth century. The Kentish Register for November 1795 reports,

"When erecting national barracks, for accommodating the military, in preference to quartering them upon the publicans, had been sanctioned by parliament, various permanent buildings of this description were begun in different parts of the kingdom, exclusive of numerous temporary constructions for the same purpose, during the present war".

Barracks of this early phase were built in places where there would regularly be a major military presence; on the Scottish borders, at embarkation points and in London. Elsewhere the innkeepers and publicans continued to provide the army with food and accommodation until the military reforms of the 1870's.

The Kentish Register reports that the first occupants of the new Canterbury Cavalry Barracks, the New Romney Light Dragoons, moved in on October 1st 1795. In the latter years of the Napoleonic wars an infantry barracks was built on the city side of the cavalry barracks. Later in the century they were joined by the insertion of an artillery barracks.

The barracks witnessed frenetic activity during the Second World War; this was to continue after the war as the depot became a centre for National Service training. The suspension of National Service in 1957 triggered the demise of the historic barracks. By the end of the 1960's all the historic buildings, bar the old garrison theatre (now a sports centre) and the church, had been demolished. The last reminder of the military presence on the site is a small T.A outfit: it is swamped by council housing and office blocks.

The Officers' House

The so called "new" riding school, which dates from 1881, is the only building that remains of the handsome Combermere Barracks. The group of refined early nineteenth century barracks survived until the early 1960's when the MOD, ever keen to improve, saw fit that they should be replaced.

The Combermere Barracks, previously known as either the Spital or Cavalry barracks, were built in 1804 for the Household Cavalry. First occupied, at the request of George III, by the Royal Horse Guards (The Blues), the barracks, periodically, became the home also to the 1st and 2nd lifeguards. After regimental amalgamations they housed the Lifeguards and the Blues and Royals. Their loss is particularly regrettable.

The Barrack Block

The clock that once sat proudly in the central pediment of the Officers' Mess is the only surviving remnant of the Brigade of Guards' 1876 Cardwell barracks. In 1980 the Victorian barracks were vacated and put to piece-meal use while their future was discussed. Though the original plan had been to restore the old barracks, the discovery that it would cost less to build afresh led to their demolition. In 1985 the old Victoria Barracks were levelled. The only historic structure to avoid the bulldozers was the perimeter wall. However it too was soon demolished as severe damage caused by falling trees during the 1987 storm led to a further finance based decision. The new Victoria Barracks were built on the site in 1989.

In the early 1970's further cuts in the military saw the reduction of the 1870's Cardwell depot at Reading to a quarter of its original size. Most of the notable buildings on the site, such as the officers' mess and the barrack blocks have been preserved by virtue of their falling within the area retained by the military, however, the regimental gardens, gymnasium, married quarters and countless other Victorian buildings were lost in the ensuing re-development of the area that had been released.

The grade II listed Keep, purchased by the local authority, has been put to a variety of community uses including sheltered accommodation. Regrettably, the council have spent little on maintenance and the once majestic brick building now has a dishevelled, run down appearance.

These Cardwell barracks were built from 1874-76 to house the 16th Regiment of Foot, the Bedfordshire Regiment. They served in military use for almost exactly a century. In the early 1970's the site was abandoned by the Royal Anglian Regiment and the buildings, subjected to vandalism, deteriorated with alarming rapidity. The barracks were eventually sold in 1981 to the Freemasons. Their plans to demolish the barracks met with staunch opposition from local campaigners but attempts to get the buildings listed proved unsuccessful and the vast majority of the old barrack blocks were demolished. The frontage building, standing at the head of the old drill square, was the only building to survive. Though it had its eastern wing severed off, the rest of the building was sympathetically restored to occupational use. It is now the Bedfordshire Masonic Centre.

Aldershot Camp in the nineteenth century

"The army descended on Aldershot in 1854. It created miles of dreariness." Nikolaus Pevsner, The Buildings of England, 1967.

Pevsner's scathing words were written at the time when Aldershot military town was in the midst of a radical rebuilding programme. Acres of Victorian brick buildings were systematically being demolished for replacement by flat-roofed pre-cast concrete structures. Pevsner informs us "The dreariness is being remedied now." Twenty five years on, many now rue the loss of the solidly built Victorian town. The 1960's buildings have appalling problems with condensation and ventilation and have proved vastly expensive to maintain. Some have had to be demolished.

In 1853 Aldershot was a pretty hamlet with a population of just eight hundred. By 1859 it had been overwhelmed by an enormous military complex of several permanent barracks and acres of wooden huts inhabited by tens of thousands of soldiers.

The 1830's and 40's had been stagnant decades in the development of the British army. The Commander-in-Chief, the highly respected, but elderly, Duke of Wellington, was against reform, and upon his death in 1852 the new Commander-in-Chief, Lord Hardinge was lobbied to implement radical improvements to the army, not least by the Prince Consort.

Top of the agenda was the establishment of a base to train large numbers of soldiers. A summer of thorough research in 1853 found Aldershot Heath to be the most suitable site for the new base and in spring 1854 a tract of 10,000 acres of land was purchased (at £12 per acre). Building started immediately: by 1859 1,600 huts had been erected on the site. The Crimean War proved a decisive influence on the camp's building programme. The Prince Consort himself advised that government funds for the army were far more likely to be forthcoming from the in time of war, rather than peace and it was decided that a number of permanent barracks should be built. The Wellington Lines, a group of seven brick barracks to house two brigades of cavalry, infantry and artillery were thus built between Aldershot village and the hutted site.

In the 1880's and 90's, a further building programme with the intention of turning the Aldershot camp in to a complete military town, saw the replacement of the old huts with new brick barracks and the erection of schools, hospitals, gas works etc. By the turn of the century the "home of the British army" had a military population of 25,000.

Aldershot proved its worth during the Boer war; it oversaw the mobilisation, equipping and shipment of over 60,000 men within a few months of the outbreak of the conflict. Similarly, it was heavily relied upon in both World Wars. In 1945 Aldershot became the training centre for the National Service Army and housed the Mons Officer Cadet School. On the termination of National Service in 1960, the camp was handed back to the regular army. This "new" army had new demands of the camp.

Traditionally barracks were built as self contained units, designed for soldiers to train, eat and sleep on the premises. Around the central parade ground would stand barrack blocks, dining halls married quarters, workshops, stores and armouries. However, the new army had new requirements there should be a distinct geographical division between the soldier's place of work and his (or her) living quarters. On their return to Aldershot, the regular army found an old-fashioned camp with outdated buildings. Rather than convert the Victorian buildings to their new requirements, a policy decision was made to demolish the old buildings and start afresh. The process of demolition, started in 1960, lasted for over a decade. Only a handful of historic buildings survived.

DEMOLISHED BUILDINGS

Wellington Lines 1856-59

Beaumont Barracks
Willems Barracks
Warburg Barracks
Badajos Barracks
Salamanca Barracks
Talavera Barracks
Waterloo Barracks

Stanhope Lines 1887-92

Barossa Barracks
Buller Barracks
Albuhera Barracks
Corunna Barracks
Jerome & Scott-Moncrieff Married Quarters
Maida Barracks
McGrigor Barracks
Mandora Barracks

Marlborough Lines 1890's

Blenheim Barracks
Oudenarde Barracks
Ramillies Barracks
Malplaquet Barracks
Tournai Barracks
Military Detention Centre
Connaught Hospital (main entrance still survives)
R C Church of St Michael & St Sebastian
Government Siding - Field Stores

HISTORIC BUILDINGS STILL STANDING

Smith Dorrien House
Guardroom of the Royal Pavillion
Cambridge Military Hospital
S.E District HQ, Steeles Rd
Garrison Church of All Saints 1863, P C Hardwick
Beaumont Barracks Riding School

BEAUMONT BARRACKS, WELLINGTON LINES

The two groups of 1850's buildings, the earliest permanent barracks in Aldershot, were collectively known as the Wellington Lines, taking the names of his campaigns. Beaumont Barracks, formerly known as South Cavalry Barracks, were built from 1856-59. Together with the similarly designed Warburg and Willems Barracks they were erected on the south side of Wellington Avenue, facing Badajos, Salamanca and Talavera barracks.

Beaumont, Warburg and Willems, otherwise referred to as the South Camp Cavalry Barracks, were designed as independent units. Each block comprised five barrack buildings with the horses housed on the ground floor. Soldiers could reach their barrack rooms by climbing the central stairway to a veranda running along the front of the building. In addition each barrack block had an imposing officers' mess. In 1859 William Sheldrake described the facades as having "dressings of cut stone, with a handsome pediment in the centre with stone pilasters, and surmounted by a very fine carving in solid stone of the royal arms."

Though the Wellington Lines were undoubtedly Aldershot's finest Victorian Barracks, they were not spared from demolition. The only survival, the handsome Beaumont Barracks Riding School, continues in use to this day.

Troopers outside Beamont Barracks, 1893

Beaumont Barracks during construction

Beaumont Barracks in 1963, shortly before demolition

Salamanca, Badajos and Talavera infantry barracks were built along the south side of Wellington Avenue in the late 1850's. Adjacent to these were Waterloo Barracks, home of the Royal Artillery. The group, collectively known as Wellington Lines "South Camp", were designed by Thomas S Jerome. By spanning the distance between the lofty barrack blocks with iron and glass roofs, Jerome created sheltered parade squares, large enough to provide cover for a whole battalion. These unusual structures were removed in 1922, thirty six years before the complete demolition of South Camp.

Barrosa, Albuhera, Corunna, Maida and Mandora, all famous battles of the Napoleonic Wars, were the names given to the barracks of the Stanhope lines. Added to these were Buller and McGrigor Barracks and the Jerome and Scott Moncrieff married quarters. Named after J. Stanhope, Secretary of State for War 1887-92, the brick barracks were built to replace the old hutted encampment as part of the late nineteenth century directive to turn Aldershot in to a military town.

The Marlborough Lines, built at the same time, comprised five infantry barracks named after the victories of Marlborough's campaigns: Blenheim, Oudenarde, Ramillies, Malplaquet and Tournai. Both Marlborough and Stanhope Lines were flattened in the 1960's. The only survivors: Maida Gym which is still used as a gymnasium, and two single storey buildings from Oudenarde Barracks, now home to Aldershot's Military Museum.

ALDERSHOT: OTHER IMPORTANT BUILDINGS DEMOLISHED

Nineteenth century barracks were self-contained units comprising, as well as living quarters, dining halls, armouries, workshops, stores and married quarters. With the loss of the barracks at Aldershot went the amenities of the late nineteenth century "town"; schools, hospitals, sewerage works, gas works, a power station etc. Very little survived the strident demolitions of the 1960's.

Government Field Stores

The first railway line to Aldershot was built in 1865. By the end of the century further lines and connections ensured the camp's complete integration into the rail network. The Government Field Stores, vast warehouses serviced by the railway, were built in 1879. They were demolished in their centenary year.

The Church of St Michael & St Sebastian

This Roman Catholic weatherboarded church was designed for shipment to the Crimea. Consecrated at Aldershot in 1855, it burned to the ground in the late 1960's.

Connaught Hospital

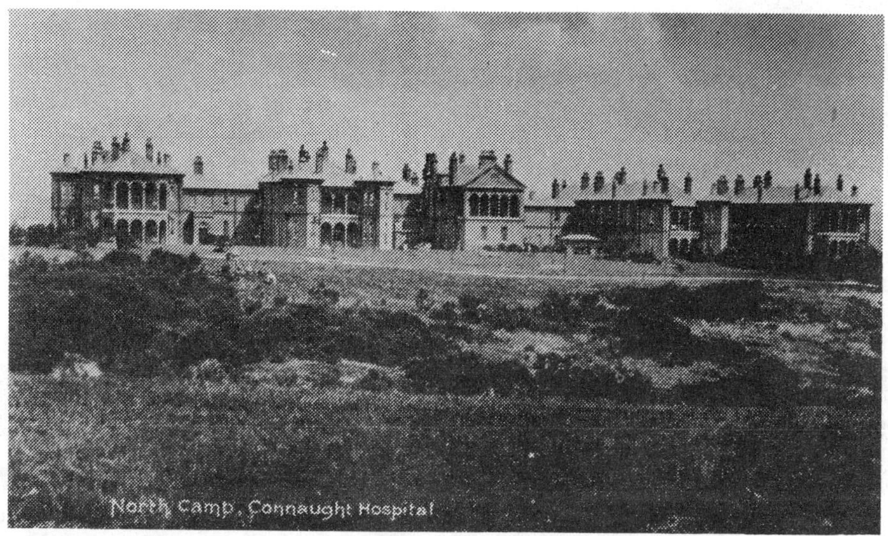

All but the main entrance of this elegant late nineteenth century barracks has been demolished over the last three years.

In addition to Maida Gym, Oudenarde buildings and the Beaumont Riding School, there are, fortunately, several interesting historic military buildings that have survived to the present day.

Guardroom to the Royal Pavilion.

The Royal Pavilion, built in 1854, was designed as a temporary residence for the Queen whilst visiting Aldershot. Lieut-Col Howard Cole writes in The Story of Aldershot (1951), that the single storey timber royal residence was "without doubt the most unpretentious of any in the United Kingdom". The Royal Pavilion was demolished soon after the publication of Cole's book. Only its guardroom survives. The now disused building, designed to accommodate a guard of eight NCO's, has the distinction of being the only remaining mid-nineteenth century timber structure in the Aldershot camp.

Smith-Dorrien House

Smith-Dorrien House was built in 1908 as a home for Methodist soldiers. The building, with its unusual fenestrated facade flanked by square towers surmounted by octagonal lanterns, is now in office use.

Cambridge Military Hospital

Cambridge Military Hospital was built in 1879 by the Aldershot builders, Martin, Wells & Co, at a cost of £45,000. The building, whose central clock turret houses the Sebastopol Bell, continues in use as a hospital.

Beaumont Riding School, now surrounded by a housing estate.

South East District Headquarters Building

The late nineteenth century building that stands at the junction of Queens Avenue and Steeles Road is a mastery of late nineteenth century ornate brickwork. It celebrates its centenary next year.

The Royal Garrison Church

All Saints, the garrison church, was built to the designs of P.C Hardwick in 1863. The contrast between the building's red brick and the yellow brick barracks that once surrounded it, gave rise to its nick name, the "red church". The barracks have long been demolished and the church now stands alone, it's 121-foot high tower a prominent landmark visible from miles around.South East District Headquarters Building

ADDISCOMBE PLACE, CROYDON

Addiscombe Place, built in 1702 as an important private residence for William Draper spent its latter years in military use. The building was design by Sir John Vanbrugh, whose staircase and salon were decorated with mythological scenes by Sir James Thornhill. Addiscombe was amongst the finest country houses of its day. During the time it was used as a private home it had many distinguished visitors, most notably King George III and William Pitt.

In 1808 the East India Company purchased the property and its estate for use as a military college. Cadets aged between fourteen and eighteen would spend two years training at Addiscombe before being sent to serve in India. Parents were required to pay fees of £50 per term, for which the the cadet would be taught mathematics, fortification, military drawing and surveying, Hindustani, French and Latin. After the Indian Mutiny of 1857-8, the East India Company which went in to rapid decline and the Addiscombe Estate was sold in 1861. Vanbrugh's house, having failed to find a buyer, was demolished. The only building left of the military site, now enveloped by the suburbs of Croydon, is an 1850's gymnasium. This, rather ostentatiously named Havelock Hall, has recently been put on the market having been converted to a number of apartments.

Recent attempts to get these Georgian barracks listed proved unsuccessful. Soon after the DoE revealed their decision against listing, they were pulled to the ground. Barracks of this date, c.1795, are extremely rare, their loss is all the more tragic.

The cavalry barracks are thought to have originally consisted of three barrack blocks, a hospital, a smithy and a riding school. Only the barracks survived to the latter part of this century, albeit in a decrepit state. The render, lined to look like stone coursing, had crumbled, exposing large areas of buff brickwork. Apparently the owners, the PSA, did make attempts to find alternative uses for the buildings, but these proved unrewarding, the chief constraint being their single depth plan. Thus Preston Barracks were lost and the historic barracks replaced by housing and a retail park.

THE VICTORIA HOSPITAL, NETLEY

The massive casulaties of the Crimean War and the army's grave lack of medical facilities led to the construction of military hospitals on a huge scale. At the request of Queen Victoria provisions were made for the erection of a new hospital in Southampton. The Queen laid the foundation stone in May 1856 and by 1863 the quarter-of-a-mile long Netley Hospital had been completed. Standing by Southampton Water, the 1,000 bed hospital treated patients brought by hospital ship from all corners of the empire.

The hospital doubled in size in 1899 with scores of wounded soldiers shipped back from the Boer war. A hutted hospital was put up to the rear of the main building. Netley witnessed similar scenes during the First World War when over 50,000 patients passed through. During the latter years of the Second World War the hospital was used by the Americans, who allegedly drove jeeps up and down the endless corridors. After their withdrawal Netley Hospital fell in to disuse. In 1966, the magnificent main building was demolished. The only historic buildings that survived were the Chapel (now a museum), the Officers' Mess (converted in to flats) and the Military Asylum (now used by the Police as a training centre).

Demolition in 1966

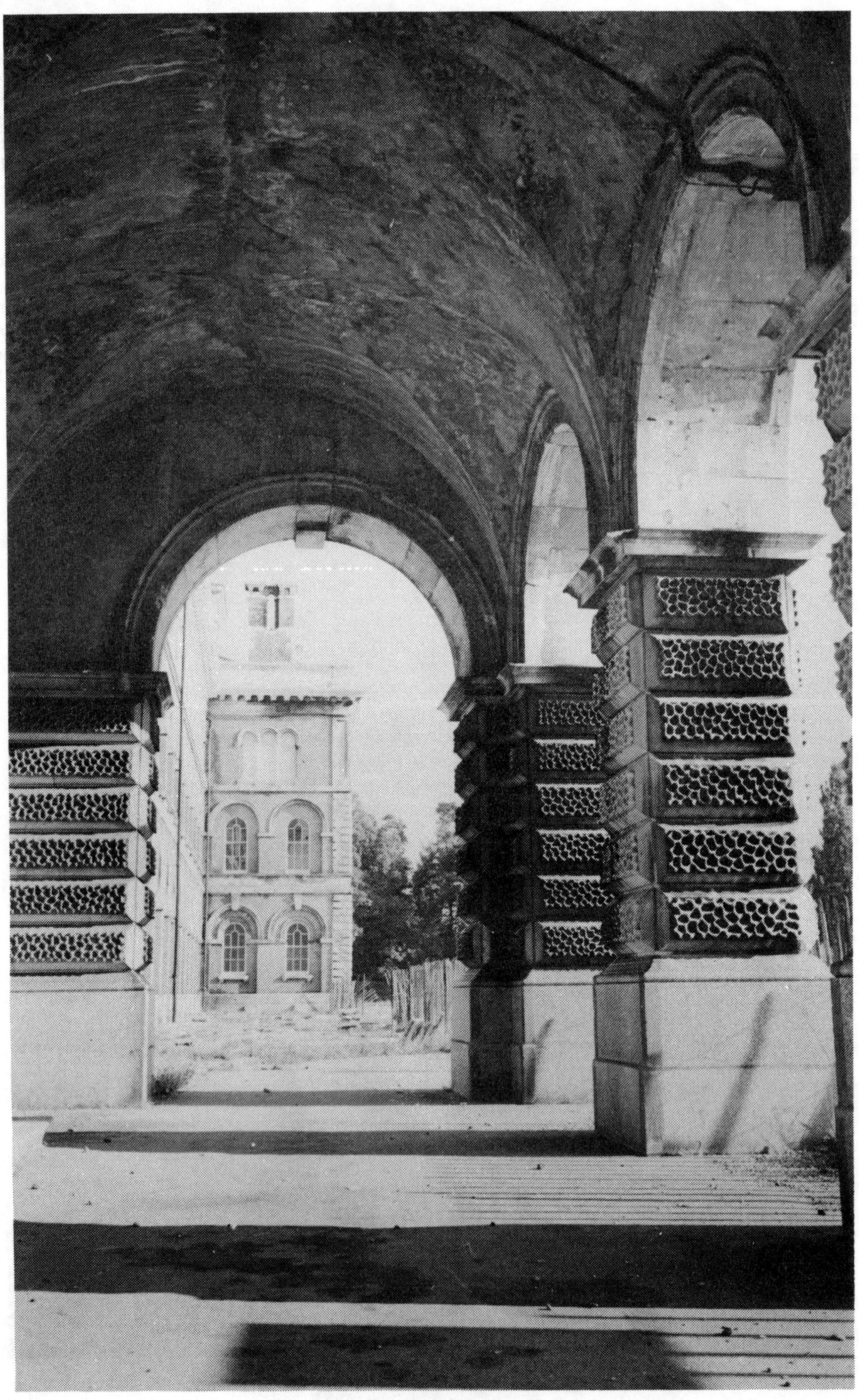

Victoria Hospital shortly before demolition

TWO IRON FRAMED SLIPHOUSES, PORTSMOUTH DOCKYARD

In 1845 Messrs Baker and Son of Lambeth were commissioned by the Admiralty to erect two all-metal slip covers at Portsmouth. The vast structures, built of cast and wrought iron with roofs of corrugated iron, were to be the forerunners of a great era of metal framed building design.

"In their employment of iron columns and arched iron trusses to support wide-spanned roofs they were pioneers, pre-dating the great station roofs at Paddington and Newcastle which are usually cited as the first examples of this form of construction"

J Coad The Royal Dockyards 1690-1850

Sadly, in 1973, the two sliphouses were demolished. The almost identical sliphouses at Chatham, which date from 1847, have, however, been preserved for posterity.

The combined efforts of German bombers and 1970's town developers saw to the eradication of at least seven eighths of the historic Clarence and Victoria Barracks. The only building to have survived, the most northerly block of Clarence Barracks, is now in use as the City Museum. The design of the grade II listed late 1890's barrack block is unusually refined, the spectacle of it standing in a quarter mile long row of similarly designed neighbours, must have been impressive. Upon the site where the infantry and artillery barracks once stood, have been erected naval married quarters, an hotel and a housing estate.

THE CRINOLINE CHURCH, ROYAL MARINE BARRACKS, EASTNEY

This delightful building was originally designed for use as a military hospital in the Crimean War from whence it was brought back to England. Here it was converted to use as a church in Havelock Park, Portsmouth. Named the Crinoline Church, because of the likeness of its silhouette to a crinoline dress, it was used as a temporary place of worship whilst the military community awaited the completion of the churches of St Simon and St Bartholomew. In the 1880's the Church was moved to Eastney where it remained as the RMA Church until the erection of St.Andrews in 1902. The Crinoline Church, which seated a congregation of up to 800 worshipers, is thought to have been demolished in about 1905.

St Vincent Barracks, built for the Royal Marines in 1847, were designed by Captain James RE. Pevsner's description of the brick built barracks was harsh. In his 1967 Buildings of England, he described the group as a "forceful, ordered composition in a debased classical style, the sort of design one would expect from an early Victorian sapper-surveyor". Within a couple of years of this damning asessment going to print, the barracks were all but demolished. The facade of the main barrack building was retained along with a small number of historic ancillary structures at the rear of the site. The re-vamped St.Vincent Barracks are now occupied by a sixth form college.

In 1807 a fire gutted Gosport's mid eighteenth century Forton Prison. In its place was constructed a fine brick and stone dressed hospital to tend to the injured returning from the Napoleonic Wars. After Waterloo the hospital was converted to use as barrack accommodation and in 1848 it became the barracks of the Royal Marines Light Infantry. It remained in such use until 1923 when they amalgamated with the Royal Marines Artillery. The Admiralty claimed that the estimated cost of £60,000 to repair the run down Forton Barracks was prohibitive and when the Royal Marines moved to headquarters at Eastney, Forton Barracks were left to decay. After several years of abandonment, they were demolished. Upon their site now stands a housing estate.

Raglan Barracks in 1880

Raglan Barracks were built in the 1850's, to the designs of Captain Fowke RE, to accommodate two regiments of the line (2,000 men and 80 officers). The barracks were demolished in the early 1970's to be replaced by Naval married quarters. Of the old barracks, only the classical gateway survived. Built of limestone with granite dressings, it now stands disused and desolate, surrounded by characterless modern residences. Though the stopping up of the consoled bracketed windows with breeze blocks has kept vandals at bay, the grade II listed building's interiors have been ruined through the collapse of its roof. In 1991 outline planning consent was granted to convert the gateway to offices but the scheme has yet to be carried out. It is hoped that plans to improve the surrounding housing estate might spur the gatehouse's owner into proceeding with its conversion or restoration.

Raglan Barracks Gateway

The last occupants of the late eighteenth century Trowbridge cavalry barracks were the Royal Horse Artillery. Cavalry had been used in the town during the Chartist disturbances of 1839. At the close of the Second World War, the RHA abandoned the depot and in due course the buildings were demolished. Their site was developed as the Bradley Road Industrial Estate. Pictured here in 1900, note that the stables were housed beneath the living quarters, common practice for cavalry barracks to this day. The occasion was the Wiltshire Regiment of Yeomanry Cavalry's final parade before their departure for the Boer War.

The University put up fierce opposition to the plans to build a barracks in Oxford on the grounds that unruly soldiers would cause trouble in their hallowed city. However, their protests were overruled and in 1876 Cardwell Barracks were built to house the Oxfordshire and Buckinghamshire Light Infantry. The regiment was based in Cowley Barracks until 1957, a year or so before they became part of the Green Jackets, through amalgamation with the Kings Royal Rifle Corps and the Rifle Brigade. The Green Jackets, based in Peninsular Barracks, Winchester had no need for the old regional light infantry centres and Cowley Barracks were sold off.

Oxford City Council bought the married quarters for use as housing for homeless families, British Telecom took over the barrack blocks and the officers' mess remained in MOD hands. Remarkably, the buildings have remained in the same ownership to this day. However, the Cowley Barracks have not survived unscathed: they suffered a major loss in the early 1960's when the keep was demolished to make room for BT lorries. The married quarters are now in a run down condition and the officers' mess stands empty, its future uncertain.

The Keep and Officers' Mess

THE MILITIA BARRACKS, GLOUCESTER

These castellated Gothic style barracks situated near the centre of Gloucester, were built for the Royal South Gloucestershire Militia from 1854-56. They were designed by Fulljames & Waller, a local architectural practice working extensively in the city. The prison, next door, was enlarged by Fulljames at the same time. The barracks stood for just over a century. In the 1960's they were demolished to be replaced by an extension of the Shire Hall.

In 1877 the first and second battalions of the 6th of foot (the Royal Warwickshire Regiment) were amalgamated. The regiments new barracks, built on a site four miles North West of Warwick, had a more flamboyant architectural style than most other Cardwell barracks. It was therefore particularly sad when in 1960, soon after the last national service recruits had departed, the buildings were demolished. Their site is now occupied by the Hampton Magna Housing Estate

Normanton Barracks, typical of the Cardwell type, were built between 1877-81 to house the amalgamated 45th foot (the Nottinghamshire Regiment) and the 95th foot (the Derbyshire Regiment). The two foot regiments became known as the Sherwood Foresters. In 1963 personnel were moved to the Nottingham HQ and the Derby site given a stay of execution, was leased to the local council for storage use. In 1984 however, the council were asked to vacate the site and the buildings were promptly demolished. The plot was sold on to developers: amongst other commercial buildings, it is now the home of a bowling alley and a Kentucky Fried Chicken takeway.

The Derby Drill Hall, built to the designs of Robert Bridgart in 1868, was used both for civic events and as a training centre for Derby's various volunteer units. It is pictured here in 1896 prior to the annual Midland Railway Ball. It was after a similar event on May 24th 1963, that a fire completely gutted the building. Though the vast metal framed structure remained standing for several years, it was sadly never restored. Derby Drill Hall was demolished in 1970.

THE MILITIA BARRACKS, ABERYSTWYTH

The Aberystwyth Barracks were built in 1869 to house the Cardigan Militia. Built of rubble stone with distinctive yellow brick quoins and dressings, they were laid out around three sides of a courtyard to the designs of Sir James Szlumper. At the end of the Second World War the barracks, no longer used by the army, were converted in to fourteen council houses.

However, Aberystwyth District Council decided to dispose of the buildings. A long period of disuse and decay led to an announcement, in the mid 1970's, that the buildings were to be demolished. SAVE contested that the barracks were worthy and perfectly capable of restoration. However, Aberystwyth District Council remained deaf to both SAVE's protestions and the campaigns of the local community, which included a petition signed by over a quarter of the town's population, and in 1979 the barracks were demolished.

J S Benest, the architect of the Norwich Drill Hall, designed his flint and red brick structure to complement the castellated medieval tower to which it was attached. The refined 1866 drill hall reached its centenary year intact but was soon after demolished due to a regrettable decision to build a roundabout on the site.

The Sobraon barracks were built in 1875 to house the 10th regiment of Foot. As with all army buildings, they have since witnessed numerous "military shuffles" having been inhabited by The Lincolnshire Regiment, The Royal Lincolnshire Regiment, The First Batallion, 2nd East Anglian Regiment and the 2nd Batallion, Royal Anglian Regiment.

In 1960 the MOD closed the barracks and handed them over to the County Council. The transaction was accompanied by a directive that the buildings should be left fallow for a period of twenty five years in case the army should need to return. They never did return and in 1975 the site was cleared. The only survivor of the subsequent redevelopment was the grade II listed keep, which is still used as a TA centre. During the Second World War, the Sobraon Barracks were inhabited by up to 5,000 men at any one time. The site is now surrounded by a sea of council houscs.

This ornately designed gothic building, constructed of multicoloured brick in 1869 to house the 7th and 8th Battalions of the Lancashire Fusiliers, has always been referred to as a barracks, though its functions were no more than that of a drill hall. Its last military use, as a TA centre, expired in the early 1960's and after a long period of disuse it was demolished. The whole site has since been redeveloped and a roundabout now encircles the spot where the barracks once stood.

Though partially built in the 1840's as the depot of the 20th Regiment of Foot, the Victorian building programme at Wellington Barracks wasn't completed until the 1870's when, under Cardwell's reforms, they became the home of the Lancashire Fusiliers. Now only the Quartermasters Store and the Lutyens War Memorial survive, the former in use as the regimental headquarters and museum. The rest of the barracks were demolished in 1969 and have long since been replaced by a housing estate. A recent attempt, by the local MP, the Borough Planning Officer and the Regimental Association, to get the historic structures listed, proved partially successful: the War Memorial now has a grade II listing status.

The decision to direct the M65 motorway through the suburbs of North West Burnley condemned a wide swathe of historic buildings to demolition. Subsequent motorway related developments have caused further losses. Amongst these can be counted Burnley's Cavalry Barracks on Westgate and the Militia Barracks on Clifton Street.

THE CAVALRY BARRACKS, WESTGATE

The Cavalry Barracks were built in 1819 at a cost of £5,500. Their date at first sight seems unlikely, Napoleon had been defeated, there was no longer a threat of invasion, indeed it was a time of relative peace, why build barracks? The answer lies in the fact that the barracks were not built as a recruiting depot, nor a direct result of a threat from abroad, they were built to quell the disquiet of the people of Burnley. Regiments of cavalry would be posted to Burnley, on a short term basis, so as to quash any rioting. The barracks ceased their military function in 1898 and were put to a great variety of purposes until their demolition 1965.

THE MILITIA BARRACKS, CLIFTON STREET

The Clifton Street Barracks, built in 1854 for the 5th Royal Lancashire Militia, saw only thirty years in military service. Whilst in civilian hands they too were put to a variety of uses, latterly as a common lodging house. years of under-maintainance led to their rapid deterioration and they were demolished in 1981.

THE CAVALRY BARRACKS, FULFORD ROAD, YORK

The York Cavalry Barracks were erected in 1796 as part of the barrack building programme that had been initiated by William Pitt in 1792. Built of brick and set around three sides of a square, they were designed by James Johnson and John Sanders, official architects to the barrack department of the war office.

Soon after the Second World War the barracks were abandoned by the military and in 1962 the local council approved plans for their demolition. The only remnants are the guard house, part of the perimeter wall and the now disused Victorian garrison church. Thankfully the splendid coat of arms of George III, that once embellished the central pediment of the officers' mess, was saved and has been re-erected outside the Eastern District headquarters building at Imphal Barracks.

Harewood Barracks gained notoriety in 1938 when Major Milner, M.P for Leeds South East, told the House of Commons that "there could not be a worse specimen of barracks for a territorial unit." Only the intervention of the war prevented their demolition, in fact their stay of execution lasted through until the mid 1960's.

The classically designed brick building had had a rich history prior to its conversion to use as a territorial army base at the beginning of this century. Built as a private residence in the 1790's, the handsome Georgian building changed hands several times before becoming the home of Leeds High School in 1877. Had it survived, the building would undoubtedly have been listed.

New Territorial Army barracks were erected in 1962 and for the next five years the old barracks were left to crumble. Major J. Milner's wish was finally granted in 1967 when the buildings were brought to the ground and buried beneath the city's inner ring road.

The Pontefract militia barracks, erected in 1871 for the West Riding Rifles Militia, saw only a short term of service for the military as the new barracks, built on the Wakefield Road in 1878 rendered the earlier ones obsolete. The old brick built depot, designed by G Malcolm at a cost of £11,000 was sold in 1890 to the Kings School, for £3,000. The school, whose long and peripatetic history allegedly dates back to the eleventh century, inhabited the old militia barracks for a century. Its departure to new premises in 1990 spelt ruination for the old depot, which was purchased by Morrisons supermarket and swiftly demolished. Attempts to list the depot proved largely unsuccessful. The stone built gatehouse was the only building to gain protection through listing, it is now used as an electricians workshop.

The castellated monastery at Tynemouth, dissolved in 1539, was adopted by Henry VIII for use as a castle. The site remained in military use until 1960. The barrack buildings, store rooms, magazines etc that once cluttered the site were demolished soon after the army's withdrawal: the priory, an ancient monument, now stands alone.

Fortunately, an uncommonly complete record of the military site in the nineteenth century exists in the form of photographs. A professional photographer, by the name of Auty, had a studio some 100 yards from the castle. Between 1870 and the turn of the century he took dozens of pictures of the castle, all from the same viewpoint. Through these images, now held at the Northumberland Records Office, we can monitor the changes made to the occupants, the Volunteer Artillery, their munitions and their buildings. In the 1880's photograph illustrated here, to the left of the priory are the 1783 barracks and to the right a magazine of 1860's build. These structures are no more.

SUNDERLAND BARRACKS

In the 1690's an Act of Parliament was passed requiring innkeepers to feed and house billeted troops and horses at a fixed daily rate. This arrangement continued until war with France at the end of the eighteenth century precipitated the massive expansion in the army and hence a spate of barrack building.

In the North East and Sunderland particularly, large numbers of troops were stationed. This was in response, not only to the threat of invasion, but to civil unrest and the seamen's strike of 1792. The new barracks were commissioned by the Duke of York, Commander of the army, in 1796.

The wooden barracks, occupying a seven acre site, housed 1000 infantrymen and three troops of cavalry. At the centre of the site, the ornate, pedimented officers' house stood flanked by two utilitarian soldiers' barracks. The latter each contained 19 large barrack rooms, housing thirty six men and 26 sergeants rooms, housing four.

After the Napoleonic wars the military contingent at Sunderland was dramatically reduced and by 1830 the soldiers' barracks had been replaced by two smaller brick buildings. The wooden officers' house was similarly replaced during the Crimean War. The barracks were in military use until the 1920's when an enlargement of the dockyard necessitated their closure. They were demolished in 1929.

These grey limestone barracks were built in 1864 for the 1st South Durham Militia. As a result of the military amalgamations of the late 1870's, the barracks became home to the Durham Light Infantry. The buildings remained in military use until the 1930's when they were purchased by the local council for use as an old peoples' home. The council did very little to the buildings by way of maintenance and by the mid 1960s the barracks were in a very run down condition. Rather than restore the historic buildings, it was resolved to demolish and build afresh. The grade II listed grey limestone gatehouse and boundary walls now overlook an unlovely modern old peoples home.

Victoria Barracks were built in 1877, as part of Cardwell's barrack building programme, to house the East Yorkshire Regiment and Militia. Military reforms of the late 1950's saw the merger of the East and West Yorkshire Regiments to form the Prince of Wales's Own Regiment of Yorkshire, and so the barracks became redundant. The military pulled out of Victoria Barracks in 1961. The buildings stood empty, deteriorating for two decades before their eventual demolition. The original plans to erect a new police headquarters on the site failed to materialise and in 1989 houses and a supermarket were erected on the ground where the barracks had once stood.

THE CAVALRY BARRACKS, BARRACK STREET, NORWICH

Norwich's red brick cavalry barracks were constructed from 1791-93 on the site of Old Pockthorpe Manor. Built around three sides of a square, the new barracks were designed to accommodate five to six troops of cavalry, roughly 350 horses and 450 men. Two attempts by the Government to close down the barracks, in 1866 and 1882, were successfully fought off and they remained in military use for over 150 years. The fate of the Cavalry Barracks was sealed in the reorganisations of the services in the late 1950's and demolition followed soon after their sale to the local council. A housing estate now occupies their site.

LADYSMITH BARRACKS, MOSSLEY ROAD, ASHTON-UNDER-LYNE

Ladysmith Barracks, built for the militia from 1841-3, were latterly to become the home of the Manchester Regiment. They became surplus to military requirements in the 1950's and were soon after sold for redevelopment. Their site was levelled for a housing development, now known as the Ladysmith Estate.

FORT VICTORIA, ISLE OF WIGHT

This early 1850's fort was known originally as Sconce Point Fort but the name was changed at the request of Prince Albert who is thought to have been involved in the approval of the plans. Fort Victoria was built as part of the defences for the west end of the Needles Passage. Cross-fire from the nearby Fort Albert and Fort Hurst provided sound protection against any foreign intrusion. Vacated by the army in 1962, the fort was sold in several parts and over the following decade it was largely demolished. Of particular architectural merit were the associated barracks, demolished in 1969. Only the waterlevel casemates have survived. Now in the ownership of the County Council, some of the casemates are leased to various individuals for use as a museum, cafe etc.

FORT GOMER, GOSPORT

Fort Gomer, constructed from 1853-8, was the first of five polygonal land forts built to defend the western approaches to Portsmouth Harbour. The design of the forts was based on a Prussian system of mutual defence, an attempt to break away from the old bastioned system of fortification. However, Fort Gomer's defences were never put to the test, through the Victorian period it was used as a barracks and training establishment. Disarmed in 1901, the fort saw only sporadic military use until its release in 1964. Fort Gomer sold at auction for £169,000, to a developer who levelled it for a housing estate.

THE YEOMANRY BARRACKS, SIDDALLS' ROAD, DERBY

Between Derby's modern railway station and its town centre lies an open area of scrub land. The area, used in recent years for little else but car parking, was the home of Derby's Yeomanry Barracks until its demolition in the late 1960's. They were built in 1860 for the Derbyshire Imperial Yeomanry Cavalry and were in military use for exactly a century. Their closure and subsequent demolition came about as a result of the regiments 1956 amalgamation with the Leicestershire Yeomanry. The wanton destruction of these centrally located barracks is particularly galling: the historic buildings would have been suited to residential conversion.

THE ORDNANCE DEPOT, DERBY

The Ordnance depot consisted of a group of important buildings design by James Wyatt in 1805. Situated on the Normanton road, there was a main armoury, two magazines, two houses for the civil department of the ordnance and two barrack blocks to house a detachment of the Royal Artillery. The site was closed in 1826 and after a long period in use as a silk mill, it was converted to a brewery. Offiler's Brewery occupied the buildings from 1877 until 1965. The brewery was then bought out by Bass, who immediately closed the historic site and proceeded with demolition. In its place there now stands a derelict supermarket put up in the 1960s.

THE OLD MILITIA BARRACKS, DEVIZES

Devizes mid nineteenth century stone built militia barracks remained in military use for just twenty three years. Taken over by the Police authorities in 1879, they later became the headquarters of the Wiltshire Constabulary. The four blocks, dating from 1856, could have converted well to housing with the parade ground forming a pleasant private courtyard surrounded by the gracious Georgian facades. The old barracks were auctioned on June the 11th 1964. In spite of their listed status, they were demolished soon after.

THE ST JOHN'S WOOD BARRACKS

St John's Wood riding school was built from 1824-5 to the designs of the Royal Engineer, Brevet Major Tylden. The much admired grade II listed building is thought to be London's oldest surviving military riding school. However, the evidence of the historic barracks surrounding it was almost totally erased in 1979. A programme to rebuild the barrack complex saw the demolition of a great number of early, mid and late nineteenth century buildings. Amongst the modern barracks of the Royal Horse Artillery stand two lonely survivors, the riding school and the mid nineteenth century officers' mess.

RESTORATIONS
&
NEW USES

The London Scottish Drill Hall is one of the finest in the country. However, the building, which has served as a Territorial Army training centre since 1886, is extremely fortunate to survived. In 1985 planning permission was granted for the erection of a new drill hall and the run down Victorian building was heading for demolition. Only weeks before the demolition, an aside by the Prince of Wales brought the architectural importance of the building to the notice of the local council and the Department of the Environment.

Within two months the building was listed, the plans to demolish were shelved and a solution was found that incorporated the most important features of the Victorian building into the new drill hall being erected nearby in Horseferry Road. The decorative ironwork of the roof and galleries was carefully dismantled and was restored whilst awaiting reconstruction. The new, smaller building uses three of the five original bays: many of the Victorian features are echoed. The new drill hall was opened in 1988 by the Honorary Colonel of The London Scottish, the Queen Mother.

The design and construction of Newhaven Fort from 1862-71 was overseen by John Charles Ardagh RE. At the onset of the building programme, Ardagh was only 22 and had been commissioned for just three years. However his fort was inventive in its design, being the first military defence structure in England to employ the use of concrete as a building material. The fort's defences were never tested as the only military action it saw came during the First and Second World Wars when it was used as a mustering point for troops.

After the disbanding of coastal defences in Britain in 1956 the fort was abandoned by the military. It was taken over by the local authority who devised a scheme to develop the site as a holiday village. However, having severely compromised the Fort's historic integrity by demolishing all the structures above rampart level and filling in much of the subterranean passagework, the scheme was dropped and the site left at the mercy of the vandals. Only in 1981 did the council take action to save the fort. A programme of sensitive restoration has brought Newhaven Fort back in to a good state of repair and it is now a thriving visitor attraction.

New Tavern Fort was built originally as an earthwork battery in 1870. Crossing fire with Tilbury fort in Essex, it defended against any enemy attempting to sail up the Thames. The fort was remodelled several times, particularly from in 1868-72 when its smooth-bore guns were replaced by rifled muzzle loaders.

Last used as a defence structure in the First World War, the site lay vacant until the 1930's when it was converted by the local authority into a public garden. However, for the forty or so years that the fort was in this use, its masonry received little attention and suffered as a result. It was only in 1975, when a local voluntary organisation started to restore the fort, that the full extent of the decay was uncovered. New Tavern Fort has since been restored, its immaculate state due to the tireless enthusiasm of the volunteers just as much as cash input.

FORT LUTON, CHATHAM

Fort Luton was constructed in the 1880's as part of a line of forts and redoubts defending Chatham from landward attack. The seven so called "concrete ring forts", built in a radius a mile or so from Chatham, replaced an earlier ring of forts built closer to the town, but rendered obsolete by the increased range of the modern artillery.

Fort Luton saw its first and last active service, as a AA battery, during the Second World War. In the decades following, the fort lay idle, becoming the playground for vandals who dismembered, thieved and daubed graffiti, ensuring the structure's rapid decline. However, following its auction in the early 1980's, the fort was rescued by a private individual who has since carried out a sympathetic conversion. Fort Luton is now a museum. Four of its sister forts have been less fortunate: they now lie in various states of ruin.

MARTELLO NO 24, DYMCHURCH

In March 1802 The Peace of Amiens bought a temporary halt to nine years of war with France. However Napoleon's expansionist ambitions caused England to declare war in May the following year. By 1805 Napoleon had massed a naval strength capable of shipping over 150,000 troops across the channel.

The French threat led to a programme of on shore defence building. Between 1805 and 1812 a chain of seventy four Martello Towers were constructed along the Kent and East Sussex coastline. The design of these circular, solidly built towers, surmounted by a single cannon, was largely based on a french designed watch-tower in Corsica. In 1794 an English attempt invade and capture Corsica had been repulsed by a small tower on Mortella Point: its single 6-pounder and pair of 18-pounder guns proved too strong a force for HMS Fortitude (74 guns) and HMS Juno (32 guns) which were eventually forced to withdraw. Only after two days of continuous bombardment was the garrison forced to surrender. The attackers, deeply impressed by the tower's performance, made sketches and drawings of its every detail.

Of the 74 martello towers built in the south east, only 25 remain. Of the survivors, most have either been converted to a new use or are now gradually deteriorating. Martello No 24 at Dymchurch is arguably the best preserved, having been fully restored as a museum piece. In 1959 it became surplus to coastguard requirements and was taken on by the Ministry of Works. On completion of the restoration programme, the building was opened to the public. It remains in the care of English Heritage.

MARTELLO NO 13, WEST PARADE, HYTHE

It is really only the circular plan of this house that gives away it's former guise. The 1930's conversion of Martello No 13 paid scant regard for the buildings historic integrity, piercing former blank walls with obtrusive windows and crowning the whole with a most inappropriate box like conservatory. The interior was treated in an equally ruthless manner, the width of the walls being reduced so as to give a greater floor space. Thankfully, approaches to historic building conversion has changed dramatically since this work was done: Martello No 13, survives as an unlucky example from a less sympathetic age.

As one would imagine by their design and purpose, martello towers are difficult to convert to residential use. The uncommonly thick walls and lack of light pose challenging problems. The 1986 conversion of Martello No 8 has succeeded in creating a comfortable residence without compromising the original structure to any great degree. In marked contrast to the severe conversion of Martello No 13 at Hythe, here the width of the walls have not been altered and the few windows are unobtrusive. Likewise, the viewing platform works in sympathy with the structure it crowns and the erection of a walkway has ensured the re-use of the original first floor entrance.

DOVER: THE WESTERN HEIGHTS

In 1794 Parliament, fearful of French invasion, voted £50,000 for strengthening Dover Castle and for building an entirely new fortification on Western Heights on the other side of the town. The aim was to threaten French lines of communication as and when they landed on the south coast. On Western Heights the whole colossal regency fortress remains largely intact, protected by huge ditches and enfiladed by massive caponiers or gun batteries.

William Cobbet was outraged by Western Heights, "More brick and stone have been buried in this hill than would go to build a neat new cottage for every labouring man in the counties of Kent and Sussex ... This is perhaps the only set of fortifications in the world ever framed for mere hiding ... it is a parcel of holes to hide Englishmen from Frenchmen."

The fortifications were carried out under Brigadier General Twiss, one of the great military engineers of the period who also worked on the defences at Gibraltar and Portsmouth Dockyard. The projecting caponiers were added in the 1860s.

Another remarkable feature is the grand shaft completed in 1807. Designed in the form of an inverted Tower of Pisa, it consists of three concentric staircases, descending to the foot of the cliff, which could rush hundreds of troops to the harbour in a matter of minutes. It has recently been restored by Dover District Council.

There are 74 Martello towers on the south east coast but the Aldeburgh Martello is unique in its design as well as being the largest and most northerly. Built from 1808-12 the Aldeburgh Martello has a quatrefoil plan, as if four towers were fused in to one. Where other martellos were surmounted by a single gun, the Aldeburgh Martello was designed for four.

The MOD sold the derelict Martello in 1931 and for a number of years it was the favourite picnicking spot of the Mitford family. In 1936 the Martello was sold on to a lady who commissioned the architect Justin Vulliamy to convert it to a studio. Vulliamy, whilst showing great respect for the historic structure, created a characterful studio by adding an innovatively designed penthouse to the flat roof. Sadly this fell into disrepair and in 1971, when the Landmark Trust started their conversion, the Fort was in a parlous state. It has since been sensitively restored and converted, in an exemplary fashion, to a four bedroomed holiday cottage. It is one of the Landmark's most celebrated and unusual properties.

Napoleon's defeat of the Austrians and the Russians in the battle of Austerlitz in 1805 prompted a justifiable rise in concern over the threat of invasion. Harwich Redoubt was one of several buildings erected as a direct result of the perceived Napoleonic threat. Situated outside the town walls high upon the hill overlooking the harbour, the redoubt could defend Harwich on the landward side and also protect against any attack from the sea. The redoubt, armed with ten 24 pounder cannon and equipped for a garrison of 6 officers and 250 men, was completed in 1810, its erection had cost just over £58,000.

For the next 100 years the redoubt underwent progressive rearmament but its defence capability was never tested. In the 1920's the local council purchased the site and built houses on the surrounding land. The redoubt was left to decay. Though it was restored to a low key use during the Second World War, it abandoned again.

In 1969 the newly formed Harwich Society set up an action group to restore the redoubt, which the previous year had been scheduled as an Ancient Monument. Dozens of volunteers helped to clear the site and carry out basic repairs. Thanks to the efforts of enthusiasts, the redoubt is now in extremely good order and is visited by many thousands of people each year.

The 1859 Royal Commission on the defence of the United Kingdom recommended that a further line of forts be built to protect Portsmouth, two miles in advance of the Fort Elson to Gomer line. Fort Fareham, built from 1861-8 was the only one, of the three recommended, to be built. Though the forts defenses were never put to the test, it remained in use as a barracks till the end of the Second World War. It became surplus to military requirements in 1965 and was sold to Fareham Urban Council. The fort's parade has since been developed as an unsightly industrial estate. Though most of the casemates have survived in use as industrial units, the fort's historic integrity has been all but lost through insensitive development.

Fort Fareham: preparations for the industrial site

This red brick and flint Palmerston fort, built in the 1860's and disarmed in 1909, has lain redundant for much of this century. When Hampshire County Council joined forces with the Royal Armouries in 1986, it was in a parlous condition. Their subsequent programme of sensitive restoration is due for completion in 1995. The Royal Armouries have ensured the Fort a secure future by installing an eminently suitable new use. An outstation of the Tower of London, Fort Nelson has become the National Museum of Artillery. Considering the number of Palmerston follies that have been demolished, that now suffer decay or have been marred by insensitive new use, Fort Nelson has been remarkably fortunate.

The threat of a French invasion in the 1860's led to Lord Palmerston's extensive defence building programme. As well as erecting several land forts at Portsmouth, provisions were made for the construction of four circular island bastions in the Solent. Spit Bank, Horse Sand, St.Helens and No Man's Land Fort, communally known as the Spithead Forts, are remarkable seabound structures of stone and brick: they have all survived to the present time.

SPIT BANK FORT

Spit Bank was last used for military purposes during the Second World War. It was largely disused until its release by the MOD in the mid 1980's. Its new owner, intent on restoring the fort to its original appearance, had first to remove a layer of guano, often up to a foot deep, which caked the Fort. With the advice and financial assistance of English Heritage and Hampshire County Council, the owner has since completed a sensitive and highly successful restoration. Spit Bank Fort, a self contained unit housing its own artesian well, forge, quarters etc has recently been opened as a museum for public viewing.

HORSE SAND FORT

Horse Sand Fort continued in MOD use, as a radar testing centre, until very recently. In March 1993 it was sold. The intentions of its new owner are not known.

NO MAN'S LAND FORT

In the recent past both St.Helen's, which stands close to the Isle of Wight, and No Man's Land Fort have been converted to residential use. No Man's Land Fort is much larger than any of the other Spithead Forts. Since its sale in the late 1980's it has undergone extensive repairs and a lavish refurbishment. Though most of the Fort has been restored to its original working state, parts have been converted to a luxury standard; it now boasts a swimming pool, a tennis court and no less than three helicopter landing pads. To the roof has been affixed an American style lighthouse. No Man's Land Fort is currently for sale.

Interior of No Man's Land Fort before (above) and after (below) restoration

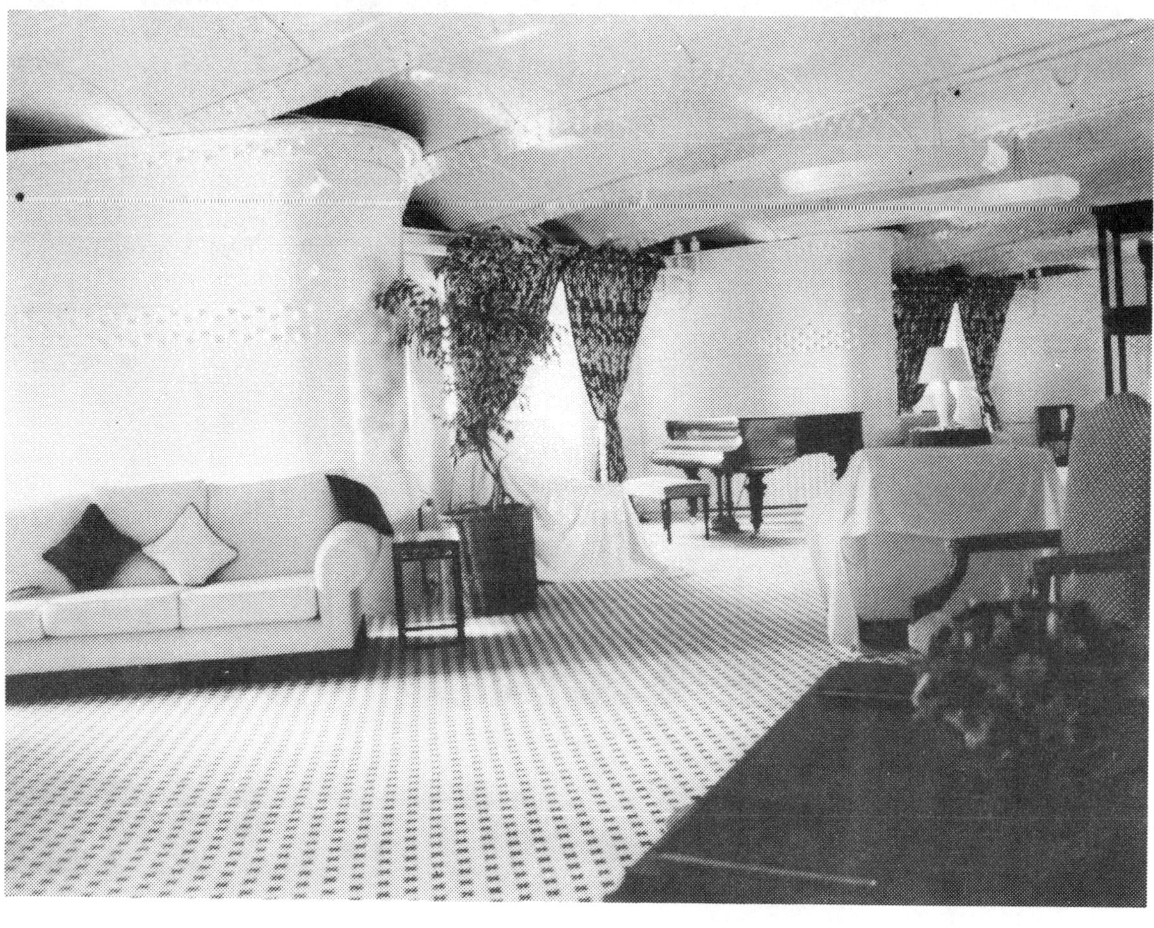

NO 10 STOREHOUSE, PORTSMOUTH DOCKYARD

The three storehouses which form the dominant architectural feature of Portsmouth's historic dockyard are described by Jonathan Coad in Historic Architecture of the Royal Navy as "arguably the most handsome of all Naval storehouses." Built from 1764-84, to house stores and equipment for the rapidly expanding fleet, the storehouses remained in their original use for two centuries.

In 1985 the Royal Navy handed over the responsibility for the upkeep of the Historic Dockyard to a trust. The Portsmouth Naval Base Property Trust receives a yearly grant to assist with the upkeep of their historic buildings and docks, which they open for public viewing. The Storehouses have all been externally restored and the clock tower of No 10 (the central) storehouse was reinstated last year. Completely destroyed by an incendiary bomb during the Second World War, the clock, its tower and cupola have all been rebuilt to their original designs.

No 10 Storehouse before restoration

No 10 Storehouse in the 1890's (above) and in the 1990's (below)

Fort Brockhurst, built in the late 1850's as part of Palmerston's defence building programme, was designed to protect Portsmouth against the threatened French invasion. The fort, built in the tradition of medieval castles, with a keep, "bailey", outer defences and a moat, became obsolete in the 1880's. However, the site remained in military use until 1958 when it was handed over to the Ancient Monuments branch of the Ministry of Public Buildings and Works. They, and their successors, English Heritage, have since carried out a rolling programme to restore the derelict fort to its pre-First World War state. The enormous task of restoring Fort Brockhurst is nearing its completion, the site is well worth a visit.

Sandown Barracks, built in the latter years of the Napoleonic War, and Sandown Battery, an 1860's Palmerston defence structure, stand on Lake Hill, either side of the main road that runs between Sandown and Shanklin. Sold by the MOD to the local authority in 1930, they have since been incorporated into a public garden. In the late 1980's South Wight Borough Council built offices and a leisure centre between the two historic structures, demolishing the two wings of the U shaped barracks, and a rare 1880's military fives court. The red and white checker bricked barracks were turned to "leisure and amenity" use. Thankfully the council now seem to have mended their ways, they recently spent £5,000 on repairs to Sandown Battery.

Sandown Barracks Battery

Fort Albert, constructed in the 1850's, was intended to stand in the sea like Spitbank Fort. It has since been connected to the land. In the 1880's the structure, also known as Cliff End Fort, was completely filled with sand as part of its conversion to use as a Brennan Torpedo launch centre. The Fort remained in the hands of the military until soon after the 1956 abolition of coastal defences, when it was sold to a private individual who emptied the structure of sand in preparation for its conversion. However, the scheme was shelved and the building remained disused for several decades. In the 1980's Fort Albert's new owners carried out a programme of restoration and completed its conversion to use as leased flats.

Golden Hill Fort was built in the 1860's as a fortified barracks for the Isle of Wight's Western defences. The hexagonal planned two storey living quarters, protected from enemy fire by the surrounding earth embankment, were surmounted by six gun emplacements each fitted with 40-pounders.

After its release by the MOD in 1962, Golden Hill Fort became home to a number of industrial outfits. A change of use in the mid eighties saw it re-open as a tourist attraction with arts and crafts shops. However, that failed to draw the number of visitors anticipated and the owners have since been looking to find a viable use for the fort. Though a small defence museum has recently been installed, the rest of the Fort is looking rather sorry. It urgently needs a suitable new use. A recent application to erect a roof to span the central area was turned down. If allowed it would have significantly altered the character and appearance of the fort.

One of the forts built on the recommendation of the 1859 Royal Commission, Crownhill, designed by Sir Edmund Frederick du Cane, was the key fort in Plymouth's landward defences. The large polygonal fort, designed for thirty two guns with accommodation for 300 officers and men, was completed in 1868.

Crownhill Fort was used by the military until 1986, one of its last tasks being as an assembly point for forces leaving for the Falklands conflict. The Landmark Trust purchased the fort and their programme of restoration is ongoing, having cleared ditches and tidied the ramparts, they are soon to tackle the restoration of the buildings. The current plan is to turn the officers' mess into a Landmark lettable property. Their approach to restoration and conversion is exemplary. Crownhill Fort, open on Monday afternoons from April to October, is well worth a visit to see a model restoration.

WOODLAND FORT, HONICK NOWLE, PLYMOUTH

Continuous use has been the key to the wellbeing of this 1860's Palmerston Fort. Though at times the fabric of the buliding has suffered from poor maintenance, basic repairs have helped to prevent serious decay. Sold by the military in 1920, the site was used for some time for rearing greyhounds before becoming home to the American army during the Second World War. After the war the Fort was taken on by the local council for use as their works depot. In 1974 Devon County Council restored the barrack block to the community use it enjoys today. Woodland Fort has become enveloped by the suburbs of Plymouth: its barracks are now used as an old peoples' lunch club, an evening social club and a branch library. The Fort's magazine is used as a ping-pong room and its other structures are used for storage. There are plans to carry out further repairs to the fort in the near future.

Picklecombe Fort, abandoned by the MOD in 1956, fortunately escaped demolition in the following years, when so much of our built heritage was lost. However, it was subjected to a somewhat heavy handed conversion (apparently admired at the time) and opened as a "boatell" in 1979

The 1861 gun battery was built at sea level: its forty two 68 and 110-pounders in two tiers and the sixteen guns on the platform, were designed to provide a barrage of wave height missiles at any foe daring to enter Plymouth Sound. The casemated battery, once described as an "on shore ship", saw little alteration in its ninety five years of service. But now the old battery, upon which two extra storeys were added, looks much like many of the 1960's high rise package holiday hotels in the Costa Del Sol.

Behind the battery stands the grandiose castellated barracks. Designed on a whim of the local landowner to look like Warwick Castle, they date from 1851. Having stood empty for many years, the barracks are now being converted to flats and it is hoped a much more sympathetic approach will prevail.

The Barracks

The Battery during conversion

The Battery converted as a hotel

This Palmerston fort, known originally as Polhawn Battery, was built from 1862-67 as part of the Plymouth defences. Polhawn, and many other forts built at the same time, never had need to fire a gun in anger: they are now often referred to as "Palmerston's Follies". However, Polhawn was put to a number of military uses, most notably as a detention cell during the First World War. The fort's chequered life in civilian hands began in 1927 when it was sold by the Ministry of War to a private individual. While in the 1930's it was turned to use as a hotel and tea rooms, after the Second World War it became a family home but suffered from poor maintenance.

In 1988 Polhawn Fort, in need of repair, was sold to John Wicksteed, a London based building contractor. Wicksteed had experience in historic building restoration, having specialised in restating Georgian and Victorian houses from flats and bedsits as family houses. The fort was suffering, particularly from damp. Five years on, after a thorough, but sympathetic restoration, the building is a thriving holiday house. The unusual self catering, eight bedroomed fort has proven to be extremely popular with group bookings. The owner, now enthused with this building type, is hoping to obtain a lease on Drake's Island in Plymouth Sound.

The Cirencester barracks, originally known as the Royal North Gloucester Militia Armoury, were built in 1857 at a cost of £8,000. The architects, Fulljames and Waller of Gloucester, built the armoury to look like an English medieval castle. The barracks ceased their military service in 1908 when the North Gloucester Militia were disbanded. Though they were used for some time as a furniture warehouse, the barracks have spent much of the century empty and disused.

However, in 1986/7 the owners, The Trustees of the Earl Bathurst Estate Settlement 1963, funded an extensive programme of repair and conversion. The grade II listed building now provides 7,300 square foot of high specification office space. Its new occupants are delighted with their historic workplace. The high ceilinged ground floor rooms have proven to be extremely successful for training as they afford ample space for overhead projection. Visiting trainees, used to working in characterless utilitarian office spaces, greatly enjoy the architecture of the historic barracks.

Parade of North Stafford Volunteers after their return from the Boer War, 1901

First mention of this red brick and stone dressed militia barracks is found in Kelly's Directory, 1850. Built for the Kings Own Staffordshire Rifle Regiment, the barracks were used by the military service for only about thirty years, since when they have housed a great variety of uses. In the 1880's part of the complex was used as a head quarters for the fire brigade; after the Territorial Army vacated the barracks in 1939, they became a centre for both the Ambulance and the Information Services. More recently under the auspices of Remploy they have housed up to eighty unemployed and disabled trainee bookbinders. They are now let to various businesses. What is remarkable is that despite all the changes of use, the grade II listed buildings have retained their mid nineteenth century character. Credit for this is largely due to the trust that has administered the site since the late nineteenth century.

The Old Militia Barracks, as they stand today

The early nineteenth century military establishment at Weedon Bec formed of three distinct elements, the Depot, the Barracks and the Pavilions. Regrettably only the depot buildings have survived.

As part of measures taken by the English Government to counter the French threat, by Act of Parliament the Government compulsorily purchased 53 acres of land at Weedon Bec for an arms and ammunition storage depot. Weedon was considered suitable because of its central location on the newly built Grand Junction Canal.

Storehouse No 14

On either side of the canal were built eight storehouses and beyond were erected the substantially built magazines. The brick vaulted double bayed magazines were built in a long line, each separated from the next by a single bayed building filled with earth. The barracks, built around a drill square, provided accommodation for units of cavalry and infantry regiments. Both the barracks and the pavilions, three grand white brick buildings, built to house the depot's governor and principal officers, were demolished in the 1960's.

The Royal Pavilion (demolished)

Between the wars the Barracks had been used as the army riding school but in the early 1960's the MOD wound down the military establishment at Weedon. A trading estate and a housing estate were built and the remaining Depot buildings passed in to civilian hands in the early 1980's.

Now the storehouses and adjacent buildings are owned by an entrepeneur involved in the building and antiques trade and they find themselves used for a great variety of purposes. The owner leases out those buildings surplus to his requirements to other companies and individuals. The whole complex is an excellent example of commercial re-use, which has brought new life to the historic buildings with few external or internal alterations.

East Lodge

The Magazines

ALMA BARRACKS, RICHMOND, YORKSHIRE

Alma Barracks, built from 1874-77 at a cost of £5,000, was the depot for the 19th Regiment of Foot, the Green Howards until 1961. On disposal, the grey granite Cardwell barracks were commandeered by the Home Office and turned in to an approved school. They remained as such until the mid 1980's when they were sold to Malcolm Tempest Ltd who designed and implemented the conversion of the barrack blocks to residential apartments and the officers' mess to an old peoples' home. The scheme, which was completed a couple of years ago has been widely acclaimed as a great success.

Comparative pictures of before and after restoration show how the architects have successfully knitted together the Howard and Hulse barracks, previously joined by an ugly pre-war addition. As a means of enhancing the central bay, an ornamented parapet was added as well as gable ends to the four projecting bays enlivening the building's silhouette. The approach to new buildings on the site showed equal respect for the old buildings, following their style in both design and building materials.

So many of Cardwell's barracks have been blighted by either demolition or disuse that Alma Barracks stand out as a rare success story.

The Officers' Mess, now an old peoples' home

The Barracks before conversion

After conversion

At Sheffield, the supermarket chain Morrisons commissioned architects the John Brunton Partnership to draw up a scheme for the conversion of the mid nineteenth century barracks. Working in sympathy with the original buildings, the architects provided 90,000 sq ft for Morrison's use and 25,000 sq ft for subletting. The drill square was turned in to a car park offering spaces for about 1,000 vehicles.

Hillsborough Barracks, built from 1848-54 at a cost of £124,000 were in military use until 1930. In civilian hands the buildings were put to a variety of uses, and general neglect led to their gradual deterioration. However, where many military buildings in a similar position have been demolished or radically altered, the Hillsborough Barracks remained largely intact. This point was not lost on the architects who strove to enhance the architectural features of the original structure. The conversion of the barracks was completed in 1992, at a cost of £12 million (96 times the cost of the mid nineteenth century building programme). The new supermarket has proved to be efficient, successful and popular: the old Hillsborough Barracks have been given a new lease of life.

Hillsborough Barracks during (above) and after (below) conversion

The North Durham Militia with their families in 1874

The grim yet imposing barracks that front on to Gilesgate were built in 1865 for the 2nd North Durham Militia. The barracks became surplus to the requirements of the military at the close of the Second World War and were soon after converted to community use. The Vane Tempest Community Centre which it has now become, continues to thrive, offering a great variety of facilities for scouts, the elderly etc. The old drill square is now used as a bowling green.

The Militia Barracks as they stand today

NOTHE FORT, PORTLAND HARBOUR

Nothe Fort dates from the 1860's and it was one of three forts built to defend the new Portland Harbour. It passed from MOD to local council control in 1961. Their plans to convert the Fort in to an hotel came to nothing and for many years it lay redundant at the mercy of vandals. In 1979 Weymouth Civic Society took on the dilapidated fort and proceeded with a programme of restoration. Nothe Fort has since been transformed into a highly successful museum and amenity centre with displays of coastal defence history, fort construction etc. It is visited by 60,000 people annually.

THE OLD MILITIA BARRACKS, KINGS ROAD, BURY ST EDMUNDS

The Old Militia Barracks were built in 1857 for the Suffolk Yeomanry. They remained in military use until 1980. Since then the site has been developed, upon the drill square now stand a cluster of sheltered houses. Fortunately grade II listed chequerwork brick built barracks avoided demolition, being sympathetically converted to residential use.

INDEX OF BUILDINGS AND SITES

SAVE would like to thank the following for their assistance in providing photographs for the exhibition and this report

*

Aldershot Military Museum, RSM J. Barlow, Jim Barnard, Tony Barrington-Hill, P. Bayldon, Bedfordshire County Council, Stuart Bingham, Bill Bolger, The Bowes Museum, Brighton Borough Council, David Brock, John Brunton Partnership Ltd, CSM M. Burrows, The Bury Times, Cambridgeshire County Council, Anthony Cantwell, Paul Carter, Chatham Historic Dockyard, David Clegg, Jonathan Coad, Peter Cobb, Cornwall Archaeological Unit, Vivien Cox, Erme Crome, R. Crowdy, Clemens Photography, Croydon Local Studies Library, Derby Museum, Keith Dobney, Barry Duffield, Durham City Council, Durham Light Infantry Museum, English Heritage, Everest, Exeter Museums Archaeological Field Unit, Jenny Freeman, Brigadier A.C Fyfe, J.L Gaines, Gloucestershire County Council, Gosport Borough Council, Mark Gray, Greater London Record Office, Great Yarmouth Society, Brigadier Hamilton Baillie, Geoff Harvey, Harwich Society, John Haynes, Ian Hook, Historic Scotland, Household Cavalry Museum, Quentin Hughes, Humberside County Council, The Independent, Lancashire Library, The Landmark Trust, The Lincolnshire Echo, Tom Lloyd, Lt.Col McIntosh, C.S Middleton, Newcastle under Lyme Library, City of Newcastle upon Tyne, The O'Shea Gallery, Oxfordshire Photographic Archive, Andrew Perry, Portsmouth City Council, QA Training Ltd, R.C.H.M.E, Richmondshire District Council, Rother District Council, Royal Borough of Kensington and Chelsea, The Royal County of Berkshire District Library, The Royal Marines Museum, The Royal Victoria Country Park Netley, Salford Local History Library, Andrew Saunders, Scarborough Borough Council, The Sheffield Telegraph, J. Smith, Victor Smith, Soldier Magazine, Suffolk Record Office, Sunderland Museum and Art Gallery, Tameside Local Studies Library, Julian Temple, Chris Tuthill, Warwickshire County Record Office, City of Wakefield Metropolitan District Council, D.J.D Wilson, Wiltshire County Council Library and Museum Service, Windsor and Maidenhead R.B.C, Gerald Wright, York City Council.

*

